GERMAN INFANTRYMAN AT WAR 1939-1945

German Infantryman at War 1939-1945

George Forty

3 1257 01553 4513

© Compendium Publishing, 2002

This edition first published by **Ian Allan
Publishing**

an imprint of Ian Allan Publishing Ltd, Hersham,
Surrey, KT12 4RG

ISBN 0 7110 2929 6

**British Library Cataloguing
in Publication Data**
A CIP catalogue record for this book is available
from the British Library

Printed and bound in Hong Kong.

Acknowledgements

This is book is heavily weighted photographically so it is to those who have very kindly allowed me to use their photographs that I must first of all address my thanks. Herr Hans-Gerhard Sandmann and I have been corresponding for the last three years, first about his late father's service in the Channel Islands and latterly encompassing the remainder of his wartime years. He was clearly a photographer of considerable skill and also one who had the great good fortune of being able to retain the results throughout the war. These now form the basis of this book. In addition, I was lucky enough, through another good friend who has helped me with my researches over a similar period—Herr Werner Wagenknecht—to discover yet another skilled photographer—Herr Erich Moog.

To these two remarkable photographers I have added a smattering of Deutsches Afrika Korps photographs, mainly from Herr Rolf Munninger and the late Colonel Ted Bock; then there is the late George Chizmar of the Real War Photos Company of Hammond, Indiana, who has supplied most of the US Army-originated photographs; Teddy Nevill of TRH Pictures supplied a lot of the Signal material; finally well-known authors Brian L. Davis and James Lucas, who have kindly allowed me to use some of their photographs. All have contributed to the wide range of diverse subjects that went to make up this glimpse of the daily life of *der Landser* in World War II. The maps were redrawn by Mark Franklin of Flatt Art.

The text to back up the photographs also originates from a number of sources, many of whom have helped me with previous books. I must thank the following individuals for allowing me to quote from their reminiscences: George Brefka, Wolfgang Everth, Hubert Gees, Guido Gneilsen, Otto Gunkel, Erwin Grubba, Horst Lueck, Agnes Mertes, Rolf Munninger, Ralph Ringler, Heinrich Stockhoff, Karl Susenberger, Werner Susek, Rolf Voelker and Werner Wagenknecht. In addition I must thank the Imperial War Museum Sound Archive for allowing me to quote from two of its tapes; also, I have drawn upon a postwar (1951) United States Army military pamphlet that covered small unit actions in Russia, now in the public domain. Mr Ron van Rijt of the Netherlands has also kindly allowed me to quote from some of his interviews with ex-German soldiers. I am also grateful to the publishers as detailed for allowing me to quote from their books. In this connection, I have tried manfully to trace the present copyright holder of *Totentanz*, which was published in 1947, without success. To all who have helped I give my sincere thanks for their considerable help. Finally I must thank Mrs Elisabeth Diekmann, Mr Lawrence Brooksby and my sons, Simon and Jonathan, for assisting with translations and all the other work that has gone into the preparation of this book.

George Forty
Bryantspuddle April 2001

Contents

The Universal Soldier

It is true to say that in 1939, *Das Heer* (the Germany Army) was among the best-trained and best-equipped armies in the world. Many might even say that it was the very best, with its high morale and excellent discipline, which owed much to a deep-seated tradition of patriotic militarism within the German nation. Its morale was undoubtedly at its highest in the years just before and just after the outbreak of World War II. This was helped by a forward looking General Staff and an entirely new way of tactical thinking enshrined in *Blitzkrieg*—Lightning War—which quickly had the armies of other nations reeling, even including the British whose tank gurus had actually helped to invent it!

However, although the German Army endeavoured to maintain its high standards throughout the long, wearisome years of war that followed, it could not do so. Partly this was because of the massive losses it sustained on the battlefields, but it was also because of the many internal and external pressures put upon its soldiers—and upon the rest of the Wehrmacht (German Armed Forces). These pressures included the moral dilemmas associated with Nazism and the military pressures highlighted by a barrage of constraints, complaints and impossible goals, from the man to whom they had sworn their allegiance, Adolf Hitler.

In the opening years of the war, everything went the way of the German Army, as it decisively beat the armies of the rest of Western Europe, conquering country after country with such apparent ease that it attained an almost mythical status. Its subsequent swift progress in the Balkans to rescue inept Italian allies, then its highly successful initial assault on the Soviet Union, even the opening gambits in the Western Desert, where the Germans had once again had to go to the aid of their Axis partner, had all gone "according to plan." However, the successes just could not last. The vast majority of the infantry, which is the backbone of any army, was still virtually unmechanised, having to march into battle, with its supply trains and supporting artillery drawn by horses. It is probably not well appreciated that the German Army in World War II utilised nearly twice as many horses as during World War I (2.7 million as against 1.4 million). Men, animals and machinery all suffered badly in the long Russian winter of 1941-42, where the vast distances and impossible conditions sapped everything— they perished just as Napoleon's army had done before them, heralding the inexorable slide to ultimate defeat. At the same time the vast might of the latest Allied partner, the United States, provided manpower, weapons and supplies in enormous quantities which the Axis simply could not match.

No nation the size of Germany could withstand the enormous losses brought about in defeats such as Stalingrad or the surrender of the Panzerarmee Afrika in Tunisia. These were followed by other serious losses during the invasions of Sicily and Italy, then of France. From late 1943 it was downhill all the way, although this does not mean that her troops were a pushover, as was shown by their tenacious defence of Normandy, extreme professionalism in retreat in Italy and the remarkable counter-attack in the Ardennes in the winter of 1944.

The stubborn retreat into the Fatherland both from the west and the east could only end in one thing—unconditional surrender, although the Führer did not live to see it, committing suicide just before the end of his Third Reich. Germany had suffered grievously from trying to fulfil the ambitions of the evil megalomaniac who ruled them, while her armed forces had taken massive casualties endeavouring to achieve the impossible and stave off defeat.

Throughout all these battles, the infantryman (*der Landser*) played a major role, as the second of the quotes at left highlights, albeit in numerous different guises. Some of these—such as the paratroopers (*Fallschirmjäger*) and mountain infantrymen (*Gebirgsjäger*)— were so different from normal infantry as to merit separate studies, but the mechanised infantry (*Panzergrenadier*), motorised (*motorisiert*) infantry and "people's" rifle divisions (*Volksgrenadier*) will be included here with the normal infantry (*Infanterie*) divisions, their story in World War II being told mainly through the words and photographs of those who actually took part.

Left: Oberfeldwebel Gerhard Sandmann, circa 1944. His evocative photographs are to be seen on many of the pages of this book, from France to Russia. He wears the normal field-grey uniform, with its dark green collar bearing the collar bars (*Litzen*) and edged with NCOs' 9mm braid (*Tresse*). (*H-G. Sandmann collection*)

Above: Sandmann's *Soldbuch zugleich Personalausweis*, or paybook which also acted as his personal identity papers. It recorded his military—and pre-military—service, any courses undertaken, medical details (such as injections given), etc. (*H-G. Sandmann*)

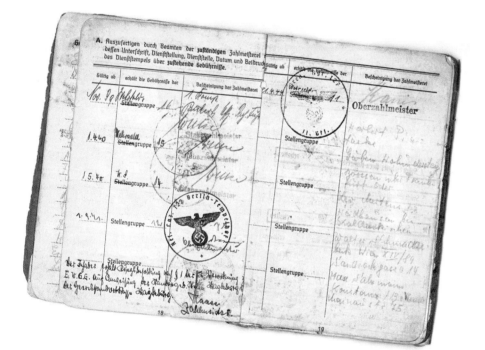

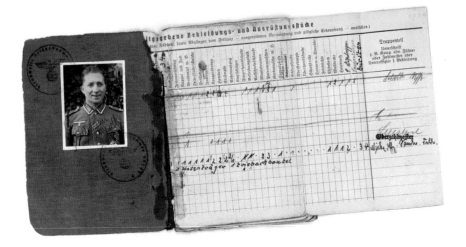

One man took many of the photographs that appear in this book. He was the late Gerhard Sandmann, who was born at Vlotho on the River Weser on 25 June 1918 and joined the German Army at Northeim in September 1939. He served as an infantry soldier from 1939 until he was captured in 1944.

His career in the infantry was no doubt very similar to that of thousands of other German soldiers—except that he survived and so did his photographic record of the places he went. He served on three fronts: in Belgium, Holland and France in 1940; Russia in 1941–42 and Northwest Europe in 1944. He was awarded the Iron Cross 1st and 2nd Class; and was steadily promoted from *Schütze* (private) up to the rank of *Oberfeldwebel* (senior sergeant major). He was wounded and spent time in hospital; he was part of the Army of Occupation in more than one occupied country (Channel Islands and France, then later in the Netherlands). Finally, he was captured by the Americans on 28 August 1944, spent time in a POW camp (in the United States) and was eventually repatriated in September 1945—possibly earlier than average—to return to civilian life.

In addition he suffered all the battlefield "norms"—such as excitement, boredom, fear, stress and privation—which went to make up the life of the "universal soldier" of World War II. What makes him somewhat special was his ability with a camera and the fact that somehow he was able to safeguard the photographs he took, so that they could provide this remarkable insight into his life as a soldier.

Of course Gerhard did not serve on every front or fight in every battle of every campaign; so, while a very large number of the photographs are from his collection, others have been included which come from the pages of similar albums belonging to other old soldiers, or from the central collections of countries—such as the US Army Archives. These have been included so as to try to show as many places and aspects of the life of the average German infantry soldier as possible.

Backing up the photographs are reminiscences and battle accounts from individual soldiers and official wartime reports. Again, these are meant to help the reader to understand all aspects of the daily life of a soldier, the bad times and the more fleeting good ones, the moments of sheer terror and those of comradeship, which was probably more than anything else the real reason why they went on fighting when everything was falling about their ears.

This book is not a tribute to war, but rather an honest attempt to explain what it was like to be a German infantry soldier during World War II.

The montage of documents on this page records various facets of Sandmann's military career and his time as a POW afterwards.

Above Left: Credit balance while an American POW.

Above Centre: Official approval of the award of the Iron Cross Second Class.

Above Right: Official approval of his wound badge.
(*All: H-G. Sandmann collection*)

Above: German telegram.

Right: Red Cross mail, passed by US censor.

Below Right: Prisoner of war tag.
(*All: H-G. Sandmann collection*)

Opposite Page: Inside views of Sandmann's Soldbuch showing hospital record (Top), movement records (Centre) and the inside cover (Below) showing stamped official photograph and signature. The pullout page on the right is his clothing and equipment record. (*All: H-G. Sandmann collection*)

Chapter 1 Joining Up

Left: Eighteen young men of "Age-Group 1921" all from the village of Gesmold, photographed on the steps of the Blue House in Melle near Osnabrück, after their *Musterung* on 14 June 1940. Heinrich Stockhoff is on the far right of the rear row. By the end of the war nine of them would have been killed or reported missing in action. (*Heinrich Stockhoff*)

Right: The military district system as at 1941.

CONSCRIPTION

From 16 March 1935 onwards, service in the German armed forces was compulsory for German citizens, so, apart from those who were already serving when this law came into force, almost everyone else was a conscript, less the few who volunteered ahead of the call-up.

The recruit, who had to be a German citizen without a criminal record, was first medically examined to ensure that he was both physically and mentally fit. Initially, standards were high; however, as the war progressed and manpower became more and more at a premium, the standards were lowered and men of lower medical grades were taken into service. For example, the 70th Infantry Division, formed in 1944, which fought extremely well in the defence of Walcheren Island, had been given the nickname of the "White Bread Division" because so many of its soldiers had stomach problems and thus needed special rations! Another example, although within the Waffen-SS, was the "Hitler Youth" Division whose 16 and 17-year olds received sweets instead of cigarettes in their rations, but were just as dangerous as their older compatriots.

DIE WEHRKREISE

The basis upon which all recruitment, drafting, induction and training was carried out in the German Army during World War II was the Military District (*Wehrkreis*) system under which the Reich was territorially organised. It also took on responsibility for the mobilisation of the divisions and the provision of trained replacements. The military districts had been established in 1919 at a time when the Treaty of Versailles limited the entire inter-war German Army (*Reichsheer*) to 100,000 men. Until 1934, there were just seven military districts outside the demilitarised zone. Prior to 1938, the military districts worked under the direct control of the Army High Command (*Oberkommando des Heeres* [OKH]). Afterwards the functions of the military districts were co-ordinated under the newly created Replacement Army (*Ersatzheer*). In 1939, there were 18 military districts divided between six army groups. Each military district was normally the administrative body for two army corps that were raised within its boundaries. These corps contained field and depot divisions as well as replacement regiments. Before general mobilisation in June 1939,

each military district had two components in its headquarters: a tactical component, which became the corps HQ in the field, and a second component that remained in the military district and was responsible for training and reinforcement. Older, less fit men unable to take part in active operations normally staffed this component.

Although this may appear at first sight to be a rigid system, it actually had considerable flexibility, as can be judged by the way that later in the war divisions were disbanded, rebuilt and even re-roled, all within the *Wehrkreis* system. It is also worth pointing out that each and every one of the original 100,000-strong peacetime army was a hand-picked officer or NCO with officer potential, who became the teaching core of the army when it expanded, so that from the outset all the new units had a leavening of battle-experienced, highly trained men. From just seven infantry divisions in 1933, Hitler was able to expand this small force into a massive 51 divisions by 1939. These were mainly infantry divisions, although they did include five tank, four motorised and three mountain divisions. This rapid expansion was managed successfully thanks largely to the expertise and enthusiasm of the 100,000 instructors of the prewar army.

MOBILISATION

The German Army was mobilised in "waves" and this process continued throughout the war until late 1944. In 1939, there were 35 "First Wave" infantry divisions, each with a strength of 17,700 all ranks. "Second Wave" divisions were similarly equipped but contained 2,460 less men. Subsequent "waves" had less and less men, and were not always as well armed. For example, the largest variation was among the "waves" called up in the winter of 1941–42 when the losses on the Eastern Front were so heavy as to make it impossible to provide sufficient matériel for existing divisions in the field, let alone provide for the newly forming ones. Shortage of artillery weapons was one of the major deficiencies at this time. In all there were 294 infantry divisions in existence during the war, some of which were disbanded or re-roled. These divisions were called up in a total of 35 "waves" (see table on page 14).

ORGANISATION

The 1939 German infantry division was not dissimilar to the Reichsheer division of 1933. For example, it still retained a replacement (*Feldersatz*) battalion, although new developments—such as a reconnaissance battalion, an anti-tank battalion and a radio company in the signal battalion—had been added. As mentioned in the Introduction, and as will be seen from the photographs, an infantry division was always very dependent upon horses for transport throughout the war. Few infantry units had many lorries or other mechanised vehicles, the exception being the *Panzerjäger* (anti-tank) companies—and, of course, the Panzergrenadiers who worked closely with the tanks and so had to be able to keep up with them.

Early in the war every infantry division contained three infantry regiments (commanded by an *Oberst* [colonel]), each consisting of three battalions (each commanded by a *Major*), an artillery regiment of three field and one medium artillery battalions, a signal battalion, an engineer battalion, an anti-tank battalion, a reconnaissance battalion and a replacement battalion.

During the war, the organisation of infantry divisions underwent two major changes and one minor one. The first was when the *Neues Art* (new style), or Type 44 division, was introduced in 1943. The main change was the reduction of infantry battalions within infantry regiments from three to two. This was inevitable because most regiments on the Eastern Front had by then lost at least one third of their manpower through casualties. Thus they became sixteen divisions, the sixteenth being the replacement/fusilier battalion.

The next major change came with the formation of *Volksgrenadier* (VGD) divisions in 1944, which had even less manpower—the fusilier battalion was now down to a single company, while one of the infantry battalions was bicycle-borne. These divisions also had a lower scale of such major weaponry as artillery and anti-tank guns, with hand-held rocket-launchers (*Panzerfaust*) replacing normal anti-tank guns. However, the new divisions had a higher than normal issue of fast-firing machine guns and machine pistols to make up for the loss of manpower. The effectiveness of the Panzerfaust in the hands of brave soldiers was proved on many occasions, and at no time more conclusively than in a verbal report on the bravery of his

ORGANISATION OF A GERMAN INFANTRY DIVISION

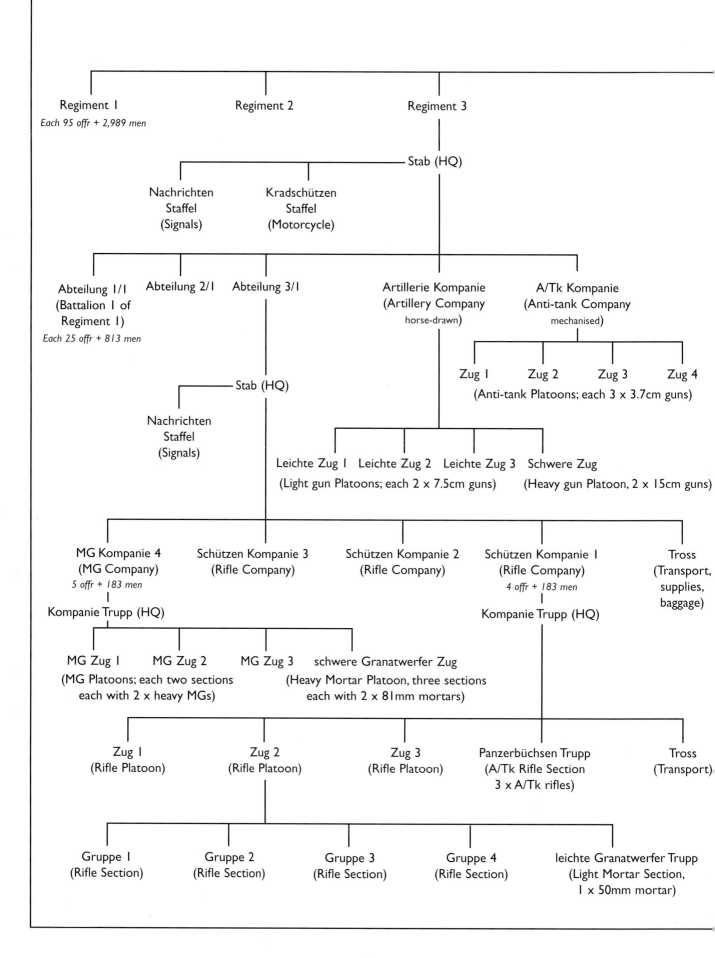

Regiment 1
Each 95 offr + 2,989 men

Regiment 2

Regiment 3

Stab (HQ)

Nachrichten Staffel (Signals)

Kradschützen Staffel (Motorcycle)

Abteilung 1/1 (Battalion 1 of Regiment 1)
Each 25 offr + 813 men

Abteilung 2/1

Abteilung 3/1

Artillerie Kompanie (Artillery Company horse-drawn)

A/Tk Kompanie (Anti-tank Company mechanised)

Zug 1   Zug 2   Zug 3   Zug 4
(Anti-tank Platoons; each 3 x 3.7cm guns)

Stab (HQ)

Nachrichten Staffel (Signals)

Leichte Zug 1   Leichte Zug 2   Leichte Zug 3
(Light gun Platoons; each 2 x 7.5cm guns)

Schwere Zug
(Heavy gun Platoon, 2 x 15cm guns)

MG Kompanie 4 (MG Company)
5 offr + 183 men

Schützen Kompanie 3 (Rifle Company)

Schützen Kompanie 2 (Rifle Company)

Schützen Kompanie 1 (Rifle Company)
4 offr + 183 men

Tross (Transport, supplies, baggage)

Kompanie Trupp (HQ)

Kompanie Trupp (HQ)

MG Zug 1   MG Zug 2   MG Zug 3
(MG Platoons; each two sections each with 2 x heavy MGs)

schwere Granatwerfer Zug
(Heavy Mortar Platoon, three sections each with 2 x 81mm mortars)

Zug 1 (Rifle Platoon)

Zug 2 (Rifle Platoon)

Zug 3 (Rifle Platoon)

Panzerbüchsen Trupp (A/Tk Rifle Section 3 x A/Tk rifles)

Tross (Transport)

Gruppe 1 (Rifle Section)

Gruppe 2 (Rifle Section)

Gruppe 3 (Rifle Section)

Gruppe 4 (Rifle Section)

leichte Granatwerfer Trupp (Light Mortar Section, 1 x 50mm mortar)

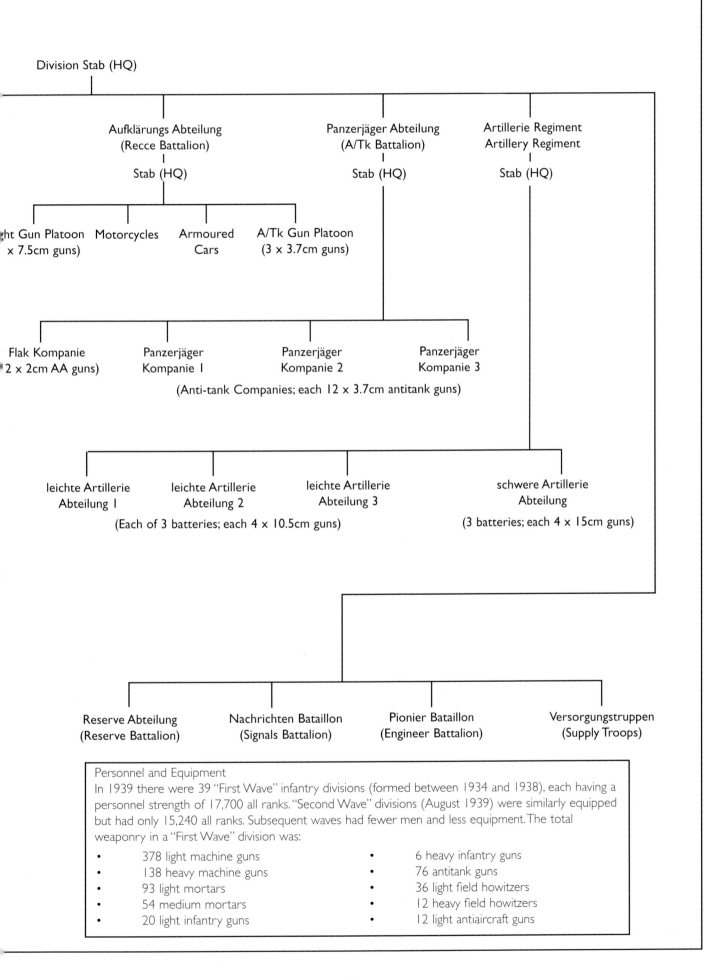

Division Stab (HQ)

Aufklärungs Abteilung
(Recce Battalion)
Stab (HQ)

Panzerjäger Abteilung
(A/Tk Battalion)
Stab (HQ)

Artillerie Regiment
Artillery Regiment
Stab (HQ)

ht Gun Platoon
x 7.5cm guns)

Motorcycles

Armoured
Cars

A/Tk Gun Platoon
(3 x 3.7cm guns)

Flak Kompanie
2 x 2cm AA guns)

Panzerjäger
Kompanie 1

Panzerjäger
Kompanie 2

Panzerjäger
Kompanie 3

(Anti-tank Companies; each 12 x 3.7cm antitank guns)

leichte Artillerie
Abteilung 1

leichte Artillerie
Abteilung 2

leichte Artillerie
Abteilung 3

schwere Artillerie
Abteilung

(Each of 3 batteries; each 4 x 10.5cm guns)

(3 batteries; each 4 x 15cm guns)

Reserve Abteilung
(Reserve Battalion)

Nachrichten Bataillon
(Signals Battalion)

Pionier Bataillon
(Engineer Battalion)

Versorgungstruppen
(Supply Troops)

Personnel and Equipment
In 1939 there were 39 "First Wave" infantry divisions (formed between 1934 and 1938), each having a personnel strength of 17,700 all ranks. "Second Wave" divisions (August 1939) were similarly equipped but had only 15,240 all ranks. Subsequent waves had fewer men and less equipment. The total weaponry in a "First Wave" division was:

- 378 light machine guns
- 138 heavy machine guns
- 93 light mortars
- 54 medium mortars
- 20 light infantry guns

- 6 heavy infantry guns
- 76 antitank guns
- 36 light field howitzers
- 12 heavy field howitzers
- 12 light antiaircraft guns

soldiers made personally by Generaloberst Erhard Raus, commander of Third Panzer Army, to the Führer in his bunker on 8 March 1945, during which Raus said: "I am able to report that during the battle in Pomerania, 580 enemy tanks were knocked out of which two-thirds—that is 380 vehicles—were destroyed by individual soldiers using the Panzerfaust. Never before has an army achieved so much success with that weapon."

Finally, in 1945 the Type 45 division came into effect. Its organisation was not unlike that of the VGD, but by that time, everything was desperate and manpower, new weapons, etc, were in even shorter supply. It was more of a paper exercise than a meaningful reorganisation and few Type 45 divisions were ever established.

MOTORISED DIVISIONS

Only four infantry divisions (2, 13, 20 and 29) were fully motorised and classified as *Infanterie Divisionen (Motorisiert)* at the outbreak of war. Later they were redesignated as Panzergrenadier divisions or converted into Panzer divisions.

MANPOWER

By the time the new VGDs were being approved the German Army had taken massive casualties on all fronts. Some 750,000 were killed, wounded or taken prisoner on the Western Front alone and many, many more in the East (the figure would rise to nearly 7.5 million by the end of the war—which means that over half the 13 million who served in the army were killed, wounded or made POW by the end of the war). To make up for some of these deficiencies, not only were the call-up age limits extended at both ends, so that they now covered all those from 16 to 60, but reserved civilian occupations were subject to careful scrutiny and the "sick, lame and lazy", the sweepings of the prisons, etc were included. This was at the "bottom" of the barrel, while at the "top", also ready to be trained as new infantrymen, were hardy sailors from the rapidly diminishing German Navy (*Kriegsmarine*)—for whom there were no ships—and *Luftwaffe* personnel, many of whom were fit aircrew without any aircraft to fly. All of this must have put considerable strain upon the training machine, yet it must have succeeded, as the VGDs on the whole fought bravely and performed satisfactorily, despite their inadequate training and experience. Within the Type 45 division there were Russian volunteers officially included who were known as *Hiwis*.

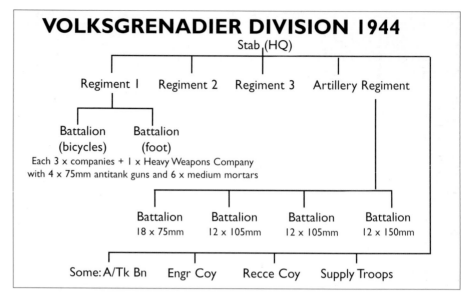

VOLKSGRENADIER DIVISION 1944

Stab (HQ)

Regiment 1 — Regiment 2 — Regiment 3 — Artillery Regiment

Battalion (bicycles) — Battalion (foot)

Each 3 x companies + 1 x Heavy Weapons Company with 4 x 75mm antitank guns and 6 x medium mortars

Battalion 18 x 75mm — Battalion 12 x 105mm — Battalion 12 x 105mm — Battalion 12 x 150mm

Some: A/Tk Bn — Engr Coy — Recce Coy — Supply Troops

MOBILISATION WAVES FOR INFANTRY DIVISIONS

Wave	Date	How Many	Comments	Wave	Date	How Many	Comments
1	1934–38	39	Peacetime units	18	late/42	8	Occupied West
2	08/39	15	Reservists	19	02/43	10+	Replacements in East
3	08/39	22	Landwehr (older personnel)	20	07/43	7	Occupied West
4	08/39	14	Reservists	21	11/43	10	Varied
5	09/39	11	Reservists	22	12/43	6	From remnants, used in West
6	10/39	6	All disbanded 1940	23	01/44	–	Grenadiers Later absorbed
7	12/39	13	Reservists				in 25th wave
8	03/40	10+	Older personnel	24	02/44	4	From reserve
9	04/40	10	1940 draft	25	02/44	6	For use in West
10	06/40	8	Disbanded 1940	26	05/44	4	Absorbed by reformed
11	09/40	10	For Russia				divisions
12	10/40	10	For Russia	27	06/44	5	From reserve
13	12/40	9	Occupied West	28	07/44	13	From personnel on leave
14	01/41	8	Occupied West	29	07/44	10+	Grenadier (later Volksgren)
15	04/41	15	Occupied West and Balkans	30	07/44	–	Grenadier brigades
16	07/41	–	Security regiments	31	08/44	12	Absorbed later by 32nd Wave
17	1941–42	9	Russia	32-35	10/44 onward		Reformed divisions as
							Volksgrenadiers; other new units

UNIFORM AND PERSONAL EQUIPMENT

All infantry soldiers wore the same basic field grey uniform, with the trousers tucked into tall, black, studded jackboots. The jacket was buttoned, with shoulder flaps, breast and side pockets and the army spread-winged eagle, clutching in its talons a circular wreath containing a swastika, above the right breast pocket. The jacket also had a dark green high collar, at least on the earlier issues. A leather belt and leather equipment were worn. Normal head-dress was the M1935 "coal scuttle" steel helmet or the field cap. Underwear consisted of "longjohns", a collarless white shirt and grey woollen socks. Important items of equipment were a canvas bread bag, canteen, gasmask in its fluted metal cylindrical case, tent square (plus tent pegs and rope), canvas pack containing washing gear, rifle cleaning kit, spare clothing, tinned rations, hand spade. Other vital items were each soldier's record of service book (kept in his jacket pocket) and identity discs (around his neck). Officers wore a similar, but much better cut, uniform of field grey and also often wore their service cap (*Schirmmütze*) as preferred headgear. Winter clothing began as just a few items (eg a double-breasted field grey greatcoat, a woollen vest, gloves and a woven cap comforter) but from

about the middle of the war a winter battle suit of warm cloth that would fit over normal field uniform (one side white, the other camouflaged), plus a fur cap, felt boots, fur lined jackets and padded trousers, were issued. Apart from this winter clothing, field uniform and equipment remained essentially unchanged throughout the war.

WEAPONRY

The total weaponry of the "First Wave" infantry division was 378 light machine guns (MG34 or MG42), 138 heavy machine guns (again MG34/42, it was the heavier tripod mounting that made the MG34/42 be classed as a heavy machine gun), 93 light mortars, 54 medium mortars, 20 light infantry guns, 6 heavy infantry guns, 76 anti-tank guns, 36 light field howitzers, 12 heavy field howitzers and 12 light anti-aircraft guns. Every infantry soldier was armed with a rifle (usually the 7.92mm Karabiner 98k) and bayonet (26cm, one-sided) and hand grenades. Weaponry improved steadily throughout the war, but the basic small arm, the rifle, remained standard. Probably the most important development was in the increase of sub-machine guns, which added greatly to firepower. On the whole, German weaponry was as good, if not better, than that of its opponents, but the supporting equipment and soldiers' uniforms were below American standards.

Above: **New recruits to Infantry Training Battalion 396, which was in** *Wehrkreis XI.* **The district capital was the city of Hanover. They are carrying "an infantryman's best friend"— his rifle (7.92mm Karabiner 98k).** (*H-G. Sandmann*)

Left: **Young Gerhard Sandmann (on the left) with another young recruits at Infantry Training Battalion 396, Northeim, soon after induction.** (*H-G. Sandmann collection*)

Above: Recruits wearing their familiar brand-new "coal-scuttle" steel helmets. Note the usual insignia—red/black/white shield on the right side and the silver eagle and swastika on the left. (H-G. Sandmann)

SOLDIERS' STORIES

Werner Wagenknecht, who now lives in Pelm, was one of the very first group of young men to be called up in 1936, and he was not very happy about having to stitch Nazi insignia onto his uniform. He also commented that he had to pass through a "very hard school" in order to become a good soldier.

"Just a few days before my 22nd birthday, I received an enlistment order telling me to report to the 12th Infantry Regiment, at the Prince Louis Ferdinand Barracks in Halberstadt, where we were issued with fatigue dress (made of canvas), given a medical examination and made to send our civilian clothes home.

"The first few weeks concentrated on getting us fit. One of the exercises was 'pull-ups' to a very high horizontal bar. I was the smallest in our group and had to jump up even to reach the bar. While I was hanging there like a sack of potatoes, the sergeant would prick me on the bottom with his sword, as I tried desperately to get my chin up over to the bar!

"Then we trained with rifles—old World War I models and we had to wear old

World War I steel helmets too, but later we got a new Karabiner (7.92mm 98k) and new helmets which were much lighter and easier to deal with. The machine gun (08/15) was also from World War I and was water-cooled; the pistol was very heavy, again from World War I.

"Marching, shooting, cleaning, washing our clothes outside in stone troughs with cold water—it was all very hard training for me—so was the sport! Swimming for example, first a long march through the town very early in the morning, in full marching order, straight up to the 10-metre diving board where you got a kick to help you off! The corporals who watched this procedure saved non-swimmers. Broken noses were treated by the medical staff, but afterwards the poor recruits were punished—the reason being that their helmet strap had not been under the chin as ordered!

"Shooting was my favourite pastime and within a few weeks I was the best at handling the machine gun and second with the rifle. Not so the heavy revolver, the recoil being just too strong for my weak wrists. After six weeks service we were allowed to walk out in the town. At the sentry box near the iron gates, the Duty

NCO controlled all, carefully inspecting cap, sword-belt, side-arm, length of trousers and cleanliness of shoes!

"Then, in the middle of November 1936, I was ordered to report to the Commanding Officer of the regiment—steel helmet, polished belt, high boots and my marksman's badge were the order of the day. I reported and was told that, because of my level of education, I had been nominated to be an officer cadet and when I refused the proposal I was threatened with a transfer to an SS unit!"

Werner would damage his legs quite badly while playing rugby later that month (they called it Kampfball [battle ball] and it was very rough indeed). He also got knocked out during his one and only time in the boxing ring! Much time was also devoted to practising the "Goose Step" which was used on the parades that were held in the town:

"As we lived in a town with a long military tradition, so there were many parades, commemorations and funeral services at which we had to march.

"In the summer of 1937, we went on manoeuvres in the Lunebergerheide. We went by train to Celle, then marched to the barracks in Hohne. We were told that our pay would be increased by a hard living allowance—enough for a daily glass of brandy for our dry throats! We began training daily at 4am in full marching order, with steel helmets, water bottles filled with chlorinated water. We had to march through woods sprayed with tear-gas to test our gasmasks."

During their training, while using tracer ammunition, they inadvertently set fire to the heathland and the fire brigade had to be called to put it out. After four weeks they marched back to Halberstadt, night marches only!

"During a break at midnight, we were given very strong coffee, mixed with rum. Then at sunrise we found a place to rest on straw, while the medical orderlies treated our blistered feet ... when we arrived back at Halberstadt there was a grandstand erected in the marketplace and we had to parade for all the generals and VIPs ... During my last three months at Halberstadt I helped the quartermaster sergeant and, at the beginning of my second year of service, I was transferred to Blankenburg to learn administration. We were allowed to travel

Above: As mentioned, some of the soldiers recruited towards the end of the war were very young. This MG42 team is from the the "Hitler Youth" SS Division, known as the "Milksop Division". If they are going to survive then they need to get their machine gun onto a Flak mounting quickly, so as to be able engage the dreaded "Jabos" (Allied fighter/ground-attack aircraft) which they appear to have spotted. (James Lucas)

to Berlin at the weekend and I used to take surplus rations (bread and sausage) to give to the war widows (from World War I)— they were very grateful and offered to do my washing in return!"

Werner was released in October 1938, as being: "unfit for further military service." He commented:

"I was quite content! Through a contact in my home town I got a job in the great German firm I. G. Farben Industrie (AGFA) … we made X-ray films, films for movie cameras (as used by the Reichs Propaganda Ministry—Goebbels) and clarifying filters for gasmasks.
"At the beginning of 1942, I was called up again and had to report to Doeblen, near Chemnitz in Saxony. The little town was crowded with civilians and no one knew where to report. First thing was a blood test—I was given the wrong blood group as I discovered later during my time as a medical orderly in Guernsey. We were

then 'thrown' uniforms and told to exchange them with other new recruits if they didn't fit. We then had to pack up our civilian clothes for them to be sent home. Next we were taken in open-topped lorries to a little village in the Erzgebirge. It was bitterly cold—snow, snow and more snow! We were detailed for duties and when the officer asked for a clerk I got a good job in the orderly room in the heated village inn! I found paper and pencil and started my quartermaster work with a pay parade. I also had a good quarter in the local bakery. The room was right up under the eaves, but the smell of fresh bread in the early mornings was compensation.
"Things soon became serious as the snow was so thick and my legs just wouldn't stand it. They swelled up so badly that I couldn't put on trousers or boots and had to be transferred to hospital in Chemnitz. Then my luck changed—a young professor from Leipzig University (he had the military rank of Medical NCO!) treated me, asked about my profession and, when

he heard that I had been working for AGFA, asked who had been my director. When I told him he said that they had been fellow students. He then said, 'A man who was qualified enough to work for my old friend will not be sent to Russia!' His diagnosis was, therefore, that I was unfit for operational service and, after my discharge from hospital, I landed up in a training camp in Suippes in the Champagne District of France, near Rheims. It was a sunny, beautiful place and I was employed painting divisional signs onto tanks— I could just sit in my bathing trunks and paint and paint!
"A young corporal who did not like my behaviour ordered me to exercise with the other troops, who were reserves for the Eastern Front—field training, close combat and obstacle course work, which included jumping into trenches wearing full marching order. The inevitable happened— my knees swelled up with blood and the poor corporal had a very unfit infantryman! When my unit went east,

"… lock stock and barrel, everything I had. So there I was with literally nothing in my pocket, a dirty shirt around my neck and a pair of boots that had been singed in the fire! Then I reported to Spandau barracks, the Grenadier depot and that was where the real hell began—a couple of weeks or so of very tough training. A lot of bullying, which took the form of fatigues, packs on your backs, rifles extended at arms' length for ages—it seemed like hours—with your arms breaking … crawling on your belly, running at the double everywhere, even with your food on your plate. There wasn't much food anyway. You spilt half of it. And you were always being bullied and chivvied in that way. And anybody who wasn't doing it was called a malingerer and threatened with courts martial and what-not. I wasn't punished badly, just puffed and blowed like everybody else. Some of the NCOs were very sadistic. I remember one who came into the barrack room at night when we had just swept it. He opened the little iron stove, took the ash pan out and scattered the ashes all over the floor. Then he shouted: 'This place looks like a pigsty—clean it up!' So we had to get out of bed and do it!"

One day, he was getting a particularly hard time from an NCO who was a *Sudetendeutsche* (in other words, he came from the Sudetenland, that part of Bohemia that was given to Czechoslovakia after World War I and then had been given to Hitler and Germany by the Munich Agreement of September 1938), whom Erwin supposed wanted to prove his German credentials: *"I said to him: 'Look you are dealing here with Reichsdeutsche. We are Berliners and we're not in a concentration camp!' That shut him up for a while."* Erwin went on to explain his training a little:

"In the morning there were usually a couple of hours square bashing. But most of the day was dedicated to rifle practice, weapon training and field exercises. Mind you, having done that already in Poland, they didn't bother with the basic things like map and compass reading. That had already been done … Then we really went to the heart of it, throwing live grenades and shooting with live ammunition, training as a platoon in the field, camouflage, fieldcraft and all that sort of thing.

I began my 'wanderings' to Brittany, Normandy and then on to Guernsey—but that's another story!"

Erwin Grubba, was born in Marienberg in East Prussia in 1925, so it was not until 1942 that he was 17 and old enough to be called up. He initially trained as a Panzergrenadier, but, after service in Russia, he returned to the west and was fortunate enough to end his service in the Channel Islands. The usual "military screening" had taken place that autumn and in the spring of 1943 he received his call-up papers. "There was no way out of it anyway," he commented in a taped interview for the IWM Sound Archive (No 010006/8), "there were no such things as conscientious objectors, so we just went and that was it … And first of all I had to do a few months in Poland with a labour battalion—the *Reichsarbeitsdienst* (RAD), which was paramilitary training as well as general sort of digging anti-tank ditches and God knows what—and guard duties."

For his RAD service he was stationed near Kutno, south of Warsaw. While there he could not fail to notice the anti-German undercurrent among the local Polish people. There were also, however, a fair number of Volksdeutsch who had been expatriated to Poland from the USSR and Romania, who naturally were much more friendly. This, too, was the period when he received the greatest amount of propaganda talk. The RAD had "regular visits from various high-ranking Nazi officials who were in brown uniforms—party members—and talked about resettlement and the German reunification of Poland. And of course SS officers too, who tried recruiting campaigns to get us into the Waffen-SS for the fighting units. That was the only period they tried to recruit us … because the German Army hardly ever bothered with indoctrination of any kind."

At the end of his RAD service in August 1943 he was given two weeks leave and went home, just in time to be bombed out by the RAF:

"But looking back, I can see how skimpy it was. We really didn't have much time. We were hardly through the basics when we were called onto the square again and an officer addressed us: 'Look lads,' he said, 'you're off on a train tomorrow going to the Eastern Front.' It was all a bit rushed but the people who taught us all had Iron Crosses so they had all been at the front line in Russia or somewhere like that. They knew what they were talking about, so I suppose it was good. But I still think we were raw greenhorns ... at least we could handle our guns. And we knew what to do and how to react to certain commands ... all they really wanted you to do was to fire your rifle and throw hand grenades—that was all you had to do! ... I was a civilian in uniform I suppose."

Oberstleutnant Karl-Gunther von Hase had joined the Reichsheer in 1936, having been accepted to become an officer. In a tape he made for the IWM Sound Archive (No 13146), he explained how:

"My career was completely normal. We served as private soldiers for the first six months but also received special training. Then we were appointed as Gefreiter, the lowest sergeant rank and after three months as Gefreiter we became Unteroffizier. I then went to the War School at Potsdam and spent nine months there being trained as a Fähnrich, then joined my unit. After two years I was appointed Leutnant—that was in 1938 and at that time they still very much honoured the traditions of the old Imperial Army, so the announcement of my appointment as an officer was given on 18 January, which was the founding date of the Bismarck Reich in 1871. Later on all these dates were coupled with Hitler's birthday on 20 April. I remember one thing from my time at Potsdam—and you must make a distinction by the way, between the War School at Potsdam and the War Academy, which is the training school for the General Staff that I also went to later on. I remember that Rommel was at that time an Oberstleutnant teaching at Potsdam. Nobody, of course, knew at that time about what he would do later, but he was already the holder of the highest decoration of the Great War—the 'Pour le Mérite,' and so he was quite a distinguished man."

Right: On a route march, 2 July 1941. One of Heinrich Stockhoff's squad has a quick drink from his water bottle as they march beside the wheatfields. Stockhoff is at the rear, partly concealed. (*Heinrich Stockhoff*)

20

Chapter 2 Training

SERVICE IN THE *REICHSARBEITSDIENST*

On 26 June 1935 a law was passed making it obligatory for all able-bodied citizens to serve up to six months in the State Labour Service. Originally this had been a simple way for Adolf Hitler to get rid of the jobless, however, it soon became the normal procedure for nearly everyone before they entered the Wehrmacht. Rolf Munninger of Fellbach was typical. He was called up in April 1940, for service in the RAD, and joined Abteilung 306-3 in Rohrbach/Holledu in Bavaria. He remembers that they had "plenty of sport and training" but they also had plenty of work! For example, they straightened and regulated the River Ilm, dug a trench in which Siemens technicians would lay a cable from Donaueschingen to Freiburg, built a dam where there had been a bridge between Breisach and Colmar, and repaired bomb-damaged flats in villages in Elsass. Then, at the end of his RAD service, he was called up for the army. Undoubtedly RAD service helped to make it easier to assimilate the new recruits, as they were used to discipline, hard work and obeying orders. On top of the time spent in the *Hitlerjugend* (Hitler Youth), to which every young German male was expected to belong—joining on 15 March in the year of his tenth birthday—the young German men were far more used to being with their "comrades" than their families, so the rigours of military service came much more easily to them. Heinrich Stockhoff recalls of those far-off days:

*"On 14 June 1940, all the young men of the age group 1921 who lived in the little village of Gesmold (3,300 inhabitants) had to go for the military medical examination (*Musterung*) at the nearby small town of Melle, between Osnabrück and Bielefeld.*

"There were 18 of us and after the examination we were told that we were all: 'kv'—kriegsverwendungsfähig—that is fit for war service. After the examination was over, we wanted to have a photograph taken of our group, so Josef Husmann and I went to see a photographer called Schneider. He took us to the Blue House at Mühlenstrasse 24—a famous old building in Melle that is still there today—and he took a group photo on the steps. Then we went to the Bockstette Inn to have something to eat. The radio was on and there was a special programme about the war in France, during which the announcer said that Paris had fallen that same day. We were very pleased to hear the news because we all thought that the war would soon be over and that we would not have to

Above Left: An essential preliminary to military service was six months in the *Reichsarbeitsdienst* (RAD). Rolf Munninger's squad in Abteilung 306-3 is seen here relaxing between strenuous work periods. (*Rolf Munninger*)

Left: Rolf Munninger's RAD squad hard at work. Everyone was required to serve in the RAD and perform hard manual labour while under strict military discipline. (*Rolf Munninger*)

go to war. How wrong we were! When the terrible war did come to an end, nine of the boys of 'Age-Group 1921' who had attended the medical examination were dead.

"Then we started to walk home and on our way we went to several of the pubs in Melle and when we arrived in Gesmold we went to the local pubs as well. Everyone was very kind to us and bought us drinks. By the evening there were only six of us left together and we went to Aloys Dratmann's farm, where his mother and her maid prepared a big meal for us. When I arrived home my father wanted to know all about the day and I told him that we were all 'kv'. The day of our examination had been a very exciting and special day for us all.

"From 29 October to 28 December, I did my service with the RAD, in Abteilung K1-196 Messingen. After we had received our uniforms we were taught how to salute. We were also taught how to dig ditches. The ground was very sandy. The boys from the big towns who had been working in shops and offices, had problems with the trench digging—but not us country boys! The work was hard and we got very little free time. We weren't allowed to go to church, not even on Christmas Day."

MILITARY TRAINING

As one might have expected of the war machine that Adolf Hitler and the Nazi Party were building, military training was, at least at the beginning of the war, long, strenuous, thorough and extremely realistic as the photographs in this chapter show. Live ammunition was routinely used on both day and night exercises, with the tacit acceptance that this would result in an "acceptable level" of casualties—a small price to pay so that the others would not only survive, but would never make the same mistakes on the real battlefield where it really mattered. Heinrich Stockhoff continues:

"My second lot of calling-up papers ordered me to report to the Kloster Kaserne (barracks) in Osnabrück on 10 March, 1941. I was posted to Infanterie-Ersatz-Bataillon 37 which was in the Winkelhausen Kaserne in Osnabrück. I was put into the first platoon of No 1 Company. My identity disc said that my blood group was 'A' and my number '1435'.

"I certainly liked the army better than the RAD. When we did well in our training our platoon sergeant, Unteroffizier Willi Kraft, allowed us to have free time—for example we went on a trip into Osnabrück city. On the first Sunday there was a church service and Feldwebel Stahlberg took all the Catholics to church. The others, who

said they didn't believe in God were taken to the kitchen. They had to peel potatoes. The next Sunday all the soldiers said they believed in God! Our priest (Wehrmachtspfarrer) was Monsignore Dr Christian Dolfen and he said goodbye to us when we had to go to the front.

"For our training we went into the Atterheide and the Everheide. The rifle range was at Eversburg. I wasn't a very good rifleman, but the first time I shot lying down and firing at a 36-ring target I managed to get 33 rings. Anyone who got 32 or over got a free afternoon holiday—this was the only time I got a free afternoon!"

BUILDING NEW DIVISIONS

Otto Gunkel, of the 272nd Infantry Division, which was one of those divisions being rebuilt as a Volksgrenadier division after having been virtually destroyed in France in August 1944, recalled:

Top: After throwing grenades—attack the enemy! (*H-G. Sandmann*)

Above: Follow-up troops then approach the enemy lines, via a convenient trench. (*H-G. Sandmann*)

"The new set-up of the division was supposed to be finished by mid-October 1944. We had come back to the old 'Cathedral Barracks' in Goslar, where the famous 'Goslarer Hunters' used to stay in the old days. The men of the 272nd Infantry Division came back there from hospital or from sick leave, into a big hall outside the main barrack area. More and more men came in every day, and we welcomed a lot of our comrades from the old units. After all the formalities were finished and we had received new clothing, we were transported by military freight train to Berlin, Doberitz, on 22 September 1944—the trip took two days and on the 24th we had a big air raid on the Berlin shunting station, but it didn't cause any casualties. In the evening we arrived at the former Olympic village of Doberitz where we met our division, which was now called the 272nd Volksgrenadier Division (VGD). Again I went to the 5th Company and the sergeant placed me in the orderly room (the office) of the company right away. We stayed there for the next five weeks, before being transported to the Eifel where we took up quarters at the former NSKK (Nationalsozialistisches Kraftfahrer Korps [Motor Corps]) school at Elstar. By the end of September, the company commander, Unteroffizier Holler, myself, two runners and a man from communications had come back.

"The new establishment of the division was supposed to be finished by mid-October. Replacements came from the air force and the navy—well-fed guys who were equipped as if it was still peace and who were not very keen about serving as infantrymen. However they had to bite the bullet and they became good and loyal soldiers. Our company went into the village of Priort at Doberitz on 2 October, where our orderly room was in the Janicke Farm. The Sarge and I shared a room to sleep. The people where we were billeted took good care of us and helped make up for our lack of rations—they even washed for us and mended our clothes. There was a cinema in the Olympic village, but it was difficult to find a seat because of the mass of soldiers ... On 23 October we received a message that our division would go into action on the Western Front and would be transported there by train in the next few days. On 30 October I was promoted to private first class, backdated to 1 October. Now I was one of the 'older' soldiers! We celebrated my promotion that evening in the farmhouse where we were billeted, and the next day we said goodbye and moved up to the front."

Rolf Werner Voelker was born in Frankenthal, Pfalz, on 4 March 1920, and at the beginning of the war was working in the armaments industry as a mechanic at

Top: More anti-tank support. Excellent close-up of the 3.7cm Pak 35/36 L/45 anti-tank gun, which was the most widely used German anti-tank gun. With AP40 ammunition it could penetrate 49mm of armour at 400 yards. (H-G. Sandmann)

Above: Covering fire being provided by the 8.1cm mortar (schwerer Granatwerfer 34), which had a

maximum range of 2,400m. The light mortar is illustrated on page 27. (H-G. Sandmann)

Right: Clipping through enemy wire was never an easy task, even with these large-sized wire cutters. Note also the stick grenade (Stielgranate 24) stuck in this soldier's belt. (via TRH Pictures)

an airfield, so was not called up immediately, only receiving his call-up papers on 5 October 1940. He recalled:

"My first stop was in the Ernest Ludwig camp in Darmstadt, posted to the 4th Machine Gun Company of the 104th Infantry Rifle Regiment ... From 1941, the regiment became a Panzergrenadier regiment ... Training was in two stages: six weeks basic training with the reserve battalion, after which we received our uniform and personal equipment, then we were sent to a combat regiment for further training on weapons and technical equipment, also to driving school for those who would drive the half-tracks. The reserve battalion consisted of three rifle companies and one machine gun company, about 1,000 men in all. In Darmstadt the camp was full. We were 16 to a room, plus an old soldier who was in charge. We slept in double-tier bunk beds with straw mattresses. Every morning when we got up we had to shake our mattresses and make up our beds—the sheets and blankets had to be really neat and tidy with no creases. If they weren't good enough to satisfy our room 'oldster', then he pulled them onto the floor and we had to make them up again and again just to give us plenty of practice!

"It is difficult to compare the men who were in the Army from 1920, the old Reichswehr army, with those who were unable to find work and had joined the newly built army in 1936 and had thus found a new occupation. However, there were good instructors from both, some of whom had modern ideas. Some had fought in the French campaign in 1940 and were against old-fashioned kinds of drill and harassment. We learned very quickly to

spot the difference between those who had been 'front-line' soldiers (ie those who had fought in battle) with 'home-only' types.

"We couldn't grumble about the food when compared with the war rations of the civilian population. We also had china dishes, plates, cups and saucers to use in the mess hall, although we had to bring our own eating utensils. There were the usual shenanigans—you had to show that your hands and fingernails were clean before you got anything to eat! The cold food ration was delivered once a day for the morning and evening meal. It was delivered by a Furier—a rations NCO—direct from the kitchen to the rooms and every man had a special place in his locker to keep this ration. Also coffee (a mixture of malt and chicory) and tea (stinging nettles and herbs). One of us fetched this from the kitchen in an aluminium can. It is said that

they put something in the tea to stop the recruits from getting too sexy—the lads called it Henkolin.

"As regards weapons, there was a shortage of the new, shorter rifle (Karabiner 98k), so we had to do our drill and basic work with the old Gewehr 98 lang ... I had a bit of good luck, they gave me a precision rifle made in 1913 with a walnut butt, and I was such a good shot with it that I won lots of time off. We also learned how to handle stick grenades. We had to bind five or six together to use against tanks by placing them under the tracks. We did the same to destroy barbed-wire fences. They were very strict about the wearing of gasmasks and they made certain that ours worked properly with some sort of irritating gas. We also had to learn fieldcraft and tactics, for example how to advance and withdraw, how to win a few metres of territory, how to lie down and get up again, even how to take an enemy position with fixed bayonets.

"One of the instructors also found a new way to harass us—he made us wade

Above: Inevitably there were always more and more route marches, with full equipment. (*H-G. Sandmann*)

Left: Old enemy tanks—like this French Somua S35—were often used as hard targets to practise on with all types of anti-tank weapons. (*H-G. Sandmann*)

Right: The 5cm leichte Granatwerfer 36 was the standard light mortar of the German Army in the early war years. Small and handy, it was gradually replaced by the 8cm Granatwerfer 42 (*Stummelwerfer*) which had been originally designed for use by airborne and other special forces. (*via TRH Pictures*)

Right: Using a field telephone. There were six field telephones in each rifle battalion's signal section, while the regimental signal section had a further 12 and there were others in the infantry gun, anti-tank and machine gun companies. (*H-G. Sandmann*)

Right: These excellent stand-mounted periscopic "scissors-type" binoculars were widely used in the German Army—and highly prized by the British and Americans. (*H-G. Sandmann*)

through a manure heap! When we got back to camp I went under the shower in my steel helmet and full uniform. There was so much dirt that you couldn't even see my ammunition pouches! After our dinner break we went back onto the parade ground for drill, still in our soaking wet clothes.

"After three weeks drill and 'spit and polish' without a break, confined to barracks, we were all waiting for the day when we would be sworn in. On the appointed day, the battalion was on the parade ground in a hollow square formation, with the band at the top. Four recruits brought the regimental flag on parade, with their 'oath finger' on the flag. Then we all took the oath: 'I swear by Almighty God ...' We were all very excited and moved. We all felt that it was a good thing that we were doing and that we were sure that we would never break our oath. Little did we know that thousands of men, women and children would lose their lives, knowing that the war was lost anyway.

"After we had learned how to salute properly, we were, for the very first time, able to leave camp. And, feeling very proud of ourselves, we went into town. We were

very disappointed to discover that the girls did not pay attention to us, the new Vaterlandsverteidigen (defenders of the Fatherland) because there were already too many men in the garrison town. And we also noticed that there were a lot of officers there as well, because we had to keep on saluting!

"After being sworn in we had more individual training, such as communications, distance measuring, shooting with pistols, machine guns and mortars. We also had to do night manoeuvres and forced marches with heavy weapons. On Sunday afternoons we were allowed to go out, but as we were very short of money all we could ever afford to buy was a cup of coffee.

"In the sixth week we were re-equipped—new uniforms, shoes, high boots, the leather of which we had to dye black, and new rifles—this time the 98k. Now we were not allowed to leave camp and were told to send our civilian clothes home. We were taught how to live in the field and how make tents out of our Zeltbahn (tent section) and we had to make them over and over again. Also, having to change our uniforms every five minutes, time after time, so as to make us obey orders instantly.

"On the night before we were due to leave the barracks for the last time, the 'Barracks Ghost' (Kasernegeist), did his rounds. In our block two of our most hated instructors got a really good hiding. Before we left, the senior sergeant (der Spiess) had us all on the parade ground to tell us that we would all be punished for what had happened, but we only laughed.

"Then, with the band leading, we marched to the railway station. With our young, high spirits we could not understand why the people standing at the side of the road watching us march by, had tears in their eyes. But they were right of course, because only half of us would come back. We passed the journey through Hessen and over the Rhine to Landau singing and telling stories—were we not the men who would rescue the Fatherland?

"When we arrived with the active regiment at Landau in der Pfalz, we began the second part of our training. It was just as hard as before, but now it had more sense of purpose. All our instructors had seen active service and they now had the job of teaching us new recruits (Grünschnäbeln)—we were going to fight the Englander!"

Chapter 3 War in the West

BLITZKRIEG

At dawn on 1 September 1939, two German army groups swept across the Polish frontier—Fedor von Bock's in the north and Karl von Rundstedt's in the south. Spearheading both army groups were two Panzer corps, their aim being to encircle the Polish Army in a gigantic pincer movement. *Blitzkrieg* (Lightning War), the new form of warfare that had so suddenly broken upon the unsuspecting Poles, was simply a tactical system that German armour expert General Heinz Guderian had perfected so as to pierce the enemy's front and then to encircle and destroy his forces. Its major elements were surprise, speed of manoeuvre, shock action from both ground and air and the retention of the initiative by the attacking force. It required all commanders at every level to use their initiative to the full.

Although it was the armoured formations which played the predominant role in the Blitzkrieg tactics, they were invariably followed up closely by the infantry, whether motorised or not, who exploited the Panzers' successes and consolidated the ground gained by the armoured formations. They were also responsible for rounding up any disorganised enemy elements that remained

on the battlefield. Despite a lack of mechanisation in the field, German infantry commanders, even at a low level, were expected to apply the principle of quick reaction and to use their initiative. Rather than discouraging dash and boldness as one might think because of their insistence on obeying orders (*Befehl ist Befehl!*—an order is an order!), it was actively encouraged, especially in those early days. This flexibility would be hampered by the long months of attrition on the Eastern Front, as the experienced subalterns and NCOs were

Above and Below: The winter of the Phoney War (1939–40) was a severe one, with deep snow covering the area of no man's land between France and Germany. Both sides carried out active patrolling and there were some casualties. The photographs show an MG34 set up to cover a patrol and the patrol approaching enemy positions. (*Author's collection*)

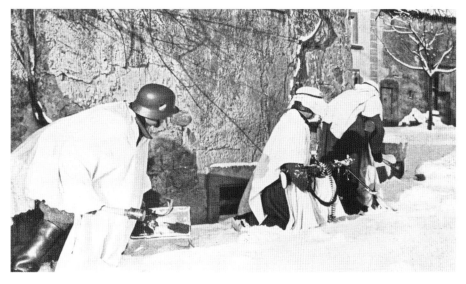

killed or promoted—so much so that offensive action almost had to be retaught for the Ardennes offensive of late 1944.

In the attack, German infantry tactics were undoubtedly marked by a skill in infiltration, small detachments penetrating between enemy posts and then engaging them from the flanks and rear with as much firepower as possible, in order to create the impression of being far stronger than they really were. They also relied upon prompt and efficient fire support from heavier weapons (mortars, infantry guns, heavy machine guns, etc) all of which were handled with great skill and elan. The degree of co-operation between this support and the riflemen of the infantry rifle platoon (*Schützenzug*) was excellent as all strove to win the firefight (*Feuerkampf*). At the same time, all arms were supported from the air by the Luftwaffe dive-bombers. Airpower formed an essential ingredient of Blitzkrieg and provided the leading troops with on-call "air artillery". Well-trained, well-led, physically fit young soldiers with high morale and an unshakeable confidence in their leaders, all this made a very potent weapon that was extremely difficult to overcome.

Even later in the war, when the going got really tough, the principle of having as much fire support as possible was maintained and the German infantry still tried to deluge the enemy with fire, to make up for their lack of numbers. Weapons such as the MG42 machine gun, probably the best general purpose machine gun of the war, the MP40 9mm sub-machine gun (by the end of the war over a million had been produced), the short-range Panzerfaust and Panzershreck anti-tank weapons, and, at close quarters, hand and rifle grenades—all were used to the fullest advantage to win the firefight. At the same time the average German infantry soldier did not like to indulge in hand to hand combat except when it was unavoidable, preferring to keep the enemy at arm's length by maintaining an intense curtain of fire.

In defence the tactic was much the same, and German infantry would also try to keep the enemy from closing by overwhelming firepower. One British commander estimated that a German infantry platoon could produce about five times as much firepower as a British one (the German MG42 had a rate of fire of up to 1,500rpm, while the British Bren Gun was only 500 rpm and the American .30 cal M1919 even less), so one needed artillery and/or armoured support to break through this dense curtain of fire.

Oberstleutnant Karl-Gunther von Hase was still a young Leutnant, acting as ADC to his regimental commander, and he remembers going with him by train to Kreuzberg in Silesia to be shown the positions they would occupy for the assault on Poland. They were part of 19th Infantry Division and he was sent to divisional headquarters on a motorcycle to collect their orders.

"I can remember that the divisional commander signed the orders and they said that the attack would begin at 0530 hours, and concluded with the words: 'God Save You!' That was how it started. Then we had the 18 days of war in Poland. My division was in the middle and was one of the six division that encircled Warsaw—later some part of each of these divisions held a big parade in Warsaw in front of Hitler down one of the main street. And the fighting was, if I can compare it to later experiences, not very hard and we did not have very heavy losses."

The Polish campaign was the first time in which he saw action and the first time he saw a dead soldier: "The first dead human body I saw in my life was a Polish Uhlan cavalryman in a colourful bluish-red uniform on a little hill in Poland. That is the sort of thing one never forgets—he was a private soldier not an officer." Another of his vivid memories of those days was of a Polish cavalry regiment that had been caught in a swamp, trying to break out of an encirclement. "As I told you, we were very fond of horses and here a whole Polish cavalry squadron was trapped in a swamp and it was terrible to listen to the last moaning of the horses—which is something a horse very seldom does—a terrible noise."

PHONEY WAR

After Germany had conquered Poland and divided the spoils with the Soviet Union, there followed a strange period of inaction on the Western Front before she launched her assault on the Low Countries and France. The British Expeditionary Force had arrived in France during September 1939, but was not allowed to occupy the Dyle Line—the Allied main defensive position in Belgium—as the Belgian Government thought that such a provocative act might upset the Germans! The French pulled back to the Maginot Line, one French general commenting: "We do not wish to fight in their territory [ie in Poland]. We did not ask for this war. Now that the Polish question is liquidated we have gone back to our lines."

The "Phoney War" continued on the Western Front, throughout the winter and spring of 1939–40, punctuated by patrolling and other such activity. However, there was action on other fronts, in particular in Scandinavia, where in February 1941, the Germans invaded Denmark and Norway, occupying them

both. Denmark immediately capitulated, but Norway put up such spirited resistance that the Allies were able to assemble an expeditionary force and send it to Trondheim. It was, sadly, an unmitigated shambles from start to finish and an Allied evacuation was ordered on 8 June, by which time events had been completely overshadowed by the news from the Western Front.

ATTACK IN THE WEST!

At 0535 hours on 10 May 1940, Germany launched *Fall Gelb* (Case Yellow), the invasion of Western Europe. German armies invaded Holland, Belgium and Luxembourg, then rapidly moved on to France in a lightning campaign that left the Allies reeling back in disarray. In just a few short weeks France surrendered unconditionally, while the British Expeditionary Force made a miraculous last-minute escape from Dunkirk and various other Channel ports. The "Little Ships" saved many of the men, but left most of their precious heavy weapons, vehicles and equipment behind on the beaches. One German Panzergrenadier observer recalled:

"During the morning our Luftwaffe appears. While the morning mists hang over the Meuse, our aircraft set to work on the southern bank, with bombs of all calibres to knock out French bunkers, infantry and artillery positions. We now know that the opposition was not of the first quality. One could almost feel sorry for the lads over

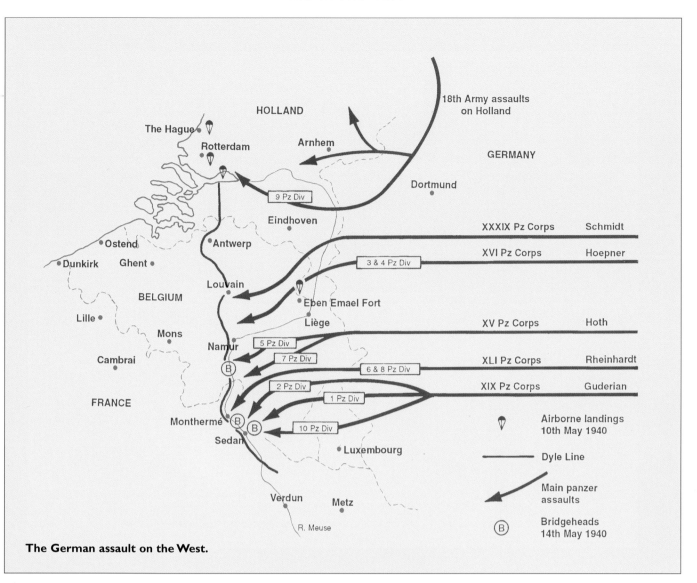

18th Army assaults on Holland

HOLLAND

The Hague

Rotterdam

Arnhem

GERMANY

9 Pz Div

Dortmund

Eindhoven

XXXIX Pz Corps · Schmidt

Ostend · Antwerp

XVI Pz Corps · Hoepner

Dunkirk · Ghent

3 & 4 Pz Div

Louvain

BELGIUM

Eben Emael Fort

Lille

Liège

XV Pz Corps · Hoth

Mons

Namur

5 Pz Div

XLI Pz Corps · Rheinhardt

Cambrai

7 Pz Div

6 & 8 Pz Div

2 Pz Div

XIX Pz Corps · Guderian

FRANCE

1 Pz Div

Monthermé

10 Pz Div

Sedan

Luxembourg

Airborne landings
10th May 1940

Dyle Line

Main panzer assaults

Verdun · Metz

Bridgeheads
14th May 1940

R. Meuse

The German assault on the West.

there. Our Panzers, riflemen and motorcycle-mounted riflemen advance out of the forests north of the river. Of course the French artillery is not going to miss such a target, but the gunners have good reason to look skywards as fresh Luftwaffe squadrons fly in to bomb them ... At 1600 hours the great attack across the whole front line is breaking loose. The divisional staff has moved to Bosseval-et-Briancourt. Air activity intensifies. On the opposite side of the river things are getting very uncomfortable. Stukas howl through the night sky, diving onto the enemy, while high above them the wings of our fighters are flashing in the sun. It is surprising how quiet the French airforce are ... By now the battle is in full swing. Enemy artillery is hammering at 2nd Panzer Division, firing at Donchery and the railway embankments to the north. Our Panzers fire into the slits

Left: Covered by a supporting gun crew, German infantrymen make an unopposed river crossing during the early stages of their Blitzkrieg on the west. (*Author's collection*)

Above: Gerhard Sandmann has acquired a horse and certainly looks to be a competent rider, as he and other members of his battalion pause en route to Antwerp. (*H-G. Sandmann*)

Above Left: Carrying rubber boats down to the next water obstacle— clearly this time there is enemy opposition. (*Author's collection*)

Left: Following behind the leading tanks, infantry carefully search damaged buildings for enemy stay-behind parties. (*Author's collection*)

Below Left: "For you the war is over!" A mixture of Allied soldiers, some walking wounded, are marshalled together by their captors. (*Author's collection*)

Right: "Marching Westward." This evocative painting shows the "ordered chaos" of just a fraction of the German Army, all trying to get to the Channel coast as quickly as possible. (*via TRH Pictures*)

Above: Singing helped you to forget your aching feet! (*H-G. Sandmann*)

Above Left: Bicycle-mounted infantry cross a hastily repaired bridge on the way through Belgium. (*H-G. Sandmann*)

Left: Some villages and towns had been heavily shelled or bombed by Stukas. (*H-G. Sandmann*)

of the bunkers. We miss our heavy artillery, but are consoled by the news that 1st Panzer Division is moving smartly forward. At 1900 hours some of our riflemen have crossed near Donchery. They reach the southern bank by swimming. Some use inflatable rafts. It is a very tough fight with considerable losses—but the bridgehead is secured ... The result of the evening: we have crossed the Meuse with all three divisions."

The German attack was well co-ordinated, every element playing its allotted role, the flak gunners, for example, destroying over 150 British and French aircraft in the bridgehead area, as the Allies strove desperately to stem the German advance:

"One by one the leading aircraft were shot to pieces, another burst into flames, a third fell about as if it was drunk. They were forced to jettison their bombs. We see parachutes floating down in the sky. Our soldiers stand up in groups on the river bank staring skywards. No one thinks of taking cover. The only danger is from crashing aircraft or jettisoned bombs."

By working through the night, building ferries they got the leading tanks across. By first light the combined bridgehead made by 1st Rifle Regiment and the Regiment

Grossdeutschland on its left, measured some three miles wide by six miles deep.

Amongst those who were involved in the German assault across the Meuse was Feldwebel Schulze, whose platoon had come under heavy, accurate artillery fire as it approached the river and had, for the first time in the campaign, been ordered to dig in. He was very relieved when he saw a flight of Ju87 Stuka dive-bombers appear and watched them bomb some of the troublesome French guns. His platoon was in a large water meadow that extended in front of them, down to and then across the river for some 800 metres, up to the higher ground where the enemy was dug in. When they started to advance towards the river bank, they soon found that they were in water almost up to their knees, which made the going extremely difficult, as did the continuing enemy fire which whipped over their heads as they struggled forward. "Barbed wire is cut through," he recalled, "and we move on ahead. In the next second everything breaks loose. Machine gun bursts whistle over us, there are strikes before, near and behind us. The enemy is shooting well." So accurate was the enemy fire that it was soon impossible for the platoon to get forward to the river. If they tried to move then they attracted more and more fire. Soon they could do nothing but lie in the water-soaked grass, hugging the

Above: Troops stop for a welcome hot meal from this horse-drawn field kitchen, parked in a convenient farmyard. (H-G. Sandmann)

Right: They shall not pass! A light machine gun detachment practise firing out into the Channel with their MG34, one of the many supporting positions in what will later become Hitler's "Atlantic Wall". (via TRH Pictures)

ground and thanking their lucky stars that the meadow grass was so tall that it made it very difficult for the enemy to see them.

Some 400 to 500 metres over to their right was another platoon, commanded by an Oberfeldwebel SP, which had managed to advance to within some 80 metres of the river, but they were also under heavy enemy fire and it was virtually impossible for any of them to move forwards or backwards.

Then, unexpectedly, "over to the right appear engineers, men hard as iron, who bring up assault boats. Oberfeldwebel SP decides to risk it with the engineers." He and two of his men leapt into one of the boats. In a few seconds the boat was in the water and they were paddling furiously towards the far shore. More followed, but the enemy artillery adjusted onto this new threat and some of the boats were blown out of the water. In the end, some 10 to 12 infantrymen, including the intrepid "SP," made it and closed on an enemy bunker, which had already been damaged by friendly fire. One of them went inside and rooted out the defenders.

Once the bunker was taken they put out strips of white material as a recognition device to stop their own supporting infantry guns firing at them. Nevertheless, even having got across the river this was the only success the company had at this particular crossing place and they were pinned down for the rest of the night.

Elsewhere, however, other German infantry were managing to cross, then to deal with the enemy bunkers, rooting out the occupants with hand grenades. One

German soldier recalled later that the enemy were: "smoked out by hand grenades; they are completely vanquished; they come out. Their faces reveal the psychological strain of this fighting. Close to each other they stand with their backs to their bunker and raise their hands."

Despite the problems that Feldwebel Schulze and his men had during their earlier attempts, they did get across the next day and soon reached the heights above Thelonne. This was where the French artillery that had given them such a hard time the day before was positioned. "We found their artillery positions left as if they had fled," recalled Schulze, "some of the guns were still loaded; the enemy had not time even to render the weapons unserviceable."

TO THE CHANNEL AND EVEN FURTHER

"After forced-marching from Lys in Belgium, via Caen, we reached the Channel in the Cherbourg neighbourhood. This was the end of the continent. We were enchanted by the glorious view of the sea. Now we were sure that the marching was nearly over. Our battalion was allotted the western section of Cherbourg, over to the well-known lobster port of Goury and in the south down to the Cap du Flamanville. The companies lay spread out far from each other in this lovely district with its steep coast, falling in picturesque shapes to the

sea, and its shimmering white bays, where the water, crystal-clear and snow-white sand invited us to bathe."

This lyrical description of the Normandy coast was written by an infantry major—Dr Albrecht Lanz who commanded a battalion in the 216th Infantry Division. When he first saw the wonderful Channel coastline he had little idea that he would have the privilege of commanding the very first German infantry unit to set foot upon British soil, in that his battalion would be chosen to spearhead the advance onto the Channel Islands. Fortunately for all concerned the initial occupation was relatively bloodless, apart from some civilian casualties caused in a bombing raid by the Luftwaffe reconnaissance aircraft

Major Lanz thought that the capture of the Channel Islands would merely be the first step in the occupation of the British Isles. However, he would not stay on the islands for very long, certainly not long enough to realise that Operation Sealion would never take place. The 216th Infantry Division would be moved back to France at the beginning of March 1941, destined for the Russian Front where he would be killed. Perhaps, therefore, it is better to quote from someone who remained on the island of Guernsey for most of the war—a member of the relieving division—319th Infantry Division, destined to become the largest division in the German Army and undoubtedly the one that saw the least action. They were nicknamed the "Canada Division" by the rest of the army who were convinced (rightly as it turned out) that many of them would end up in Canadian POW camps! Werner Wagenknecht, whom

Top Right: Mixed convoy showing how many different types of appliance were impressed into use (*H-G. Sandmann*)

Above Right: Anything is better than walking, even if you travel on the outside of a Schlepper. This one is a captured Belgian Carden-Loyd (in German parlance an Artillerie-schlepper VA 601(b) and used for towing 5cm and 7.5cm Pak guns). (*H-G. Sandmann*)

Right: First glimpse of the River Seine. (*H-G. Sandmann*)

Opposite, Above: "Just a few miles to go to the coast and we mustn't get lost!" (*H-G. Sandmann*)

Opposite, Below: The sea at last! St Laurent sur Mer. Next stop, perhaps, England! (*H-G. Sandmann*)

we met in the opening section, was one of a group of reinforcements to 319 ID. A drunken sergeant in St Mâlo referred to Wagenknecht's unit as the "death squad", so he was somewhat apprehensive of the place where he was being posted—but his fears were quickly put to rest, as he recalled:

"We sailed by steamboat (the Bordeaux*) on a stormy night. British aircraft, searchlight beams and German anti-aircraft guns were our company ... Arrival in Guernsey. This lovely, sunny day in March 1942 is deep-rooted in my heart! 'Sarnia, cherie, gem of the sea, island of beauty my heart longs for thee!' The officer in charge of the harbour gave the order that we should report to the Princess Elizabeth Hospital (used as the main military hospital during the occupation). There we were thoroughly examined and told that the army medical service had applied for reinforcements and due to my civilian education I was chosen. I had no driving licence and no experience as a medical orderly but that was no problem for the medical officer."*

Karl-Gunther von Hase recalled that he was in the area of the Loire valley after hostilities had ceased in the west and that for a while they had practised for the invasion of Great Britain—Operation Sealion:

"We stayed in France after the Armistice. We were down at the Demarcation Line on the River Loire, where we had to stop because of the Armistice regulations. And we stayed there for about another two months or so in this area of the beautiful Loire chateaux, near Saumur ... And then we started some minor exercising for that so-called strategic move, Sealion—to invade Britain. The river at Saumur had very flat banks with white sand quite like a seashore, so we had a few exercises on how to get into a boat and how to get out at the other side, but we didn't go any further. Then we were brought back to our peacetime garrison area—Celle and Hanover—and we were given permission to hold a victory parade in Celle."

"THERE REMAINS ONLY ONE ENEMY"

The final OKW communique of the campaign was sent out on 25 June 1940 and said: "There are no Allies any more. There remains only one enemy: England." Undoubtedly most German soldiers, elated with the ease in which they had conquered so much of Europe, must have thought that the war would be over in a few weeks.

How wrong they were!

Chapter 4
On to Sunnier Climes

MEANWHILE IN NORTH AFRICA

Between 5 and 7 February 1941, the tiny British Western Desert Force, under the brilliant leadership of General Sir Richard O'Connor, had virtually annihilated the inept Tenth Italian Army, driving the disorganised remnants back into Tripolitania, and thus apparently ending the immediate threat to Egypt and the Suez Canal. However, Hitler was prepared to support his Axis partner and so by mid-February German troops were landing at Tripoli—these were the leading elements of the Deutsches Afrikakorps (DAK), that, under the inspirational leadership of "the Desert Fox"—General (later Generalfeldmarschall) Erwin Rommel would write its own chapter in the annals of war.

However, first of all they had to get there from Europe. That meant either a quick, but hazardous, flight in a lumbering Junkers Ju52 transport aircraft—affectionately know throughout the Wehrmacht as "Tante Ju" (Auntie Ju)—that was easy meat for any Allied fighter aircraft, or a slower, and in many ways just as hazardous, sea journey across the Mediterranean that would be contested bitterly by the Royal Navy. These two methods of transportation provided the tenuous lifeline needed to meet the continued requirement of reinforcing the DAK, as these first three reminiscences explain. Karl Susenberger, who was going out with a party of reinforcements to the 104th Panzergrenadier Regiment, DAK, in 1942 recalled:

"It was nearly midnight when we arrived in Brindisi; we immediately disembarked and were taken to our billets which were in an old Italian barracks ... then after about a week, very early one morning, we were driven by lorry out to the military airfield—this was the special moment we had all been waiting for! The fleet of Junkers Ju52s in which we would be flying to North Africa filled the airfield—an impressive sight because there must have been between 30 and 35 of them in total. We were divided into plane loads of 18 men each and then we

were marched out to our respective aircraft. First, before we got on board, kapock-filled life jackets were handed out, which we had to put on. Then we got into the plane. Fortunately I had a seat by one of the windows, so I could easily see what was going on. Who would have ever thought when we began our training just nine months ago in Brunswick, that one day we would be flying out to Africa? No one! The big aircraft taxied to the take-off runway and away we went—it certainly was a great experience. The aircraft made a fantastic sight as we flew out over the sea. After an uneventful flight of about four hours, we landed on the island of Crete. The airfield lay very close to the sea—inviting a quick bathe. I also remember that there were large oranges for sale—I'd never seen the like of such oranges before, not even in Italy and Sicily. We stayed in Crete for about four days, then we were told to get ready to move again, because the next day we would be flying on to North Africa.

"This time we had some fighter protection—just two Messerschmitt Bf110s—a bit stingy I thought for a formation of nearly 35 planes! All went well at first, but just as we got near to the African coast there was an alarm call—'Air Attack! Enemy Fighters!' Already the first tracers were whizzing through the air. The rear-gunners on the Ju52s [there was a single MG15 in an open dorsal position in the rear of the fuselage] took up the fight to help our two fighters but, in spite of their heroic efforts, the enemy planes shot down three Ju52s—three aircraft full of our comrades who would now never reach Africa. It was sobering for us lucky ones who had survived—but what would follow?"

Werner Susek, another DAK veteran, describes his journey to North Africa:

"We left our camp at Wahn, near Cologne on 27 October 1941 and went by train down through Italy, where we spent a while

Below: On their way to Africa. A group of Ju52 transport aircraft fly low over the Mediterranean to avoid British fighters. (*Rolf Munninger*)

join 10th Company in July 1942. He had a burning ambition to prove himself as he came from an old Austrian military family. He wrote in his diary:

"We are all 21-years old and full of the craziness of youth. Crazy because we have all volunteered to go to Africa and have not stopped talking about it and nothing else for weeks and weeks. We have also been unable to think about anything else either. Our imagination has been working overtime! For example what does the word 'Africa' conjure up? I know, it's balmy, tropical nights, palm trees swaying, sea breezes blowing natives on their camels, oases and of course, those wonderful tropical helmets! Oh, and I suppose a little war as well, but how can we be anything but successful? Rommel captured Tobruk just a few days ago, so it won't be long before we are in Cairo, Alexandria and the Suez Canal!

"Cairo, what a place, all those beautiful girls and us in our immaculate white tropical uniforms! The newspapers are always full of the exploits of the Deutsches Afrikakorps. Heavens, how we will enjoy that! When we get to Africa we won't just be one of the crowd—we'll really make a name for ourselves.

"Day and night we dreamt and built our castles in the air. If only we could get away from this boring, sterile place— training recruits—ugh! Most of us have already sampled the 'delights' of Russia and the bitter cold winters and have no desire to return to the filth, the freezing temperatures and Ivan. However, apart from us six optimists, no one in the barracks thought our application to serve in Africa stood an earthly chance of success.

"And then the impossible happened! Like crazy men we jumped about, hugging each other. We really were going to Africa! That evening we just sat together for a long, long time and we still couldn't really believe it. The MO gave us a thorough examination checking to see if we had any tropical weaknesses. Sadly, one had to drop out because of a slight heart murmur. How we pitied him. All of a sudden we were a special group—almost a separate caste— the 'Africans' they called us. How our young comrades envied us, while the old ones were amused by our obvious enthusiasm—but that didn't bother us. Our hearts were singing. Great adventure awaited us in Africa and we were going to make the most of it! How fortunate we were to be getting out of these antiquated grey stone barrack blocks, where the Emperor's new recruits had spent their days. At 21 I hadn't really yet found my true identity so I had nothing to lose. Youth, idealism, victory in battle, they are all such intoxicating words—And there was no one there who could offer us better ones."

Ringler was another one who had to make the dangerous journey to Africa by air, leaving Brindisi as Susenberger had done in a "Tante Ju". He recalled:

"I was in the Junkers aircraft with about 15 others, nine of whom were officers. In

Below: Inside the "Tante Ju". Passengers and crew were supposed to wear these kapock-filled life jackets. In reality, there would have been little chance of escape in view of their low-level flight. (*Rolf Munninger*)

at Bagnoli near Naples. Then we went by boat to Benghazi in a convoy, and finally got there on 24 November. The convoy consisted of two troop transport ships with two Italian destroyers protecting us. Fortunately, the Royal Navy didn't attack us, although two days out we were intercepted by British bombers, but they didn't cause any damage. However, as luck would have it our ship developed engine trouble en route, so we had to stop in at Crete for repairs to be carried out. This made it a very long journey."

Despite the danger, there was clearly a feeling of excitement when soldiers were told they were going to serve in North Africa. Most were phlegmatic about having to fight in a strange, hostile environment, but some just couldn't wait to get there—especially those reinforcements who worried that the excitement might be all over before they arrived! One such was Lt Ralph Ringler, also of the 104th Regiment, who was sent out to

Left: Most of the DAK arrived in North Africa by troopship, after a dangerous crossing from Italy. Here a crowd of soldiers wave goodbye to a boatload of their comrades about to set out from an Italian port. (Colonel T. Bock)

Below Left: Rommel made newly arrived units march around the town of Tripoli several times, both to impress the locals and also to fool the British into thinking that the DAK was much stronger than it really was. (Colonel T. Bock)

Right: The corrugated sides of one of the ubiquitous "Tante Ju," Junkers Ju52 transport aircraft. Much of the reinforcement of the DAK was by air, although Allied air assets were able to exact a heavy toll on the unwary. (via TRH Pictures)

our consternation. 'Don't worry,' he said, 'that's just German fighter cover joining us from Tobruk.'

'Haven't we had any fighter cover any of the way before then?' I asked him. 'No Leutnant, but we've been lucky. Yesterday the British shot down a complete formation of 46 Ju52s.'... Then the pilot dug me in the ribs and pointed below. We had climbed a bit higher and I could now see not only the sea below us, but also, as straight as a ruler, the North African coast and beyond it, a dazzling yellow plain—the desert! Where was Tobruk? Oh yes there it was, just a few white blobs of houses around a small bay.

"We were landing now and quickly jolted to a halt. My eyes were blinded by the glare as the door in the side of the fuselage was flung open. The pilots became very hurried ... 'Quickly out, come on hurry, we don't want to be caught with our trousers down in the desert!' We just had time to throw out our kit, mutter a few words of thanks and then the corrugated iron bird rolled off.

"Africa and the desert had received us ... 'Posted to the DAK'—that's what it said in our posting orders. We tried to orientate ourselves on the huge airfield, where aircraft took off and landed constantly. Clearly we had to get away from there as quickly as possible. Then over to the north we saw dust clouds a long way away—was it perhaps a road? Almost liquid with the heat and swearing profusely, we dragged our large officers' chests with their 'indispensable African equipment' in its direction. The chests contained mosquito nets, small and large, sheets, underwear, body belts, shirts, socks, boots and so on. And on our heads we wore the most important item—our tropical helmets— Heia Safari!"

addition, we had all our weapons and equipment stowed away. It was my first flight so I was both excited and apprehensive. It felt very strange to begin with, I had never seen the world from so high up before. The people were no more than tiny dots, the ships in the harbour looked like little toys. After that, just the endless, shimmering sea.

"The monotonous roar of the engines, the heat and tiredness—because we had made an early start—made me fall asleep. When I woke up again we were flying over the Greek islands. They were partly covered by haze, but still looked indescribably beautiful. As the water became shallower, all the islands seemed to be surrounded by a whole spectrum of colours from deepest blue to brightest green.

"The aircraft banked over and lost altitude as we approached the landing field at Maleme in Crete. On the ground below I could see piles of damaged Ju52s, which had been destroyed in the hard battles that had raged here on the island only a year ago."

Lt Ringler spent only a few hours in Crete, then flew on to North Africa:

"We flew very low, skimming over the wavetops Shamefaced and embarrassed, my friend Gunther asked the pilot if there were any lifejackets. He grinned back and explained that they would have been totally useless. We were flying low so that the RAF wouldn't see us. However, if by some mischance they did so, then any attempt at escape would be quite impossible. We couldn't climb fast enough to avoid them and if we were shot down at this altitude nobody would have time get out, so why bother with lifejackets?

"The dark green sea with its white crests, the regular drone of the engines and the heat inside 'Tante Ju' finally made me fall asleep. I awoke, confused, the sun ever more dazzling, the heat ever more powerful. My uniform stuck to me everywhere. Then I saw a flash out of the window and started—was it an enemy fighter? The pilot, who had been watching the aircraft approaching for some time was amused at

ROMMEL STRIKES

Rommel's initial orders were to use his newly-formed DAK as a blocking force (*Sperrverband*) in order to bolster up the dispirited Italians in Tripolitania and prevent any further British advances. Any ideas of the DAK advancing were firmly ruled out by the OKH—and in any case, the Italians just weren't up to it. They had all reckoned without the "Desert Fox", as Rommel quickly became called—by both sides!

On 31 March 1941, just a few short weeks after his leading troops had started to land, Rommel attacked at Mersa Brega, slicing through the opposition and causing a general withdrawal. No matter what Berlin said, Rommel and his leading elements—like so many great armoured commanders, he was right up there with his leading troops— pressed on, capturing Agedabia on 2 April and only slowing down when they ran out of fuel. As they had done in France, the Panzers spread confusion. Rommel wrote to his wife:

"We've been attacking since the 31st with dazzling success. There'll be consternation among our masters in Tripoli and Rome, perhaps in Berlin too ... We have already reached our first objective, which we weren't supposed to get to until the end of May. The British are falling over each other to get away. Our casualties are small. Booty can't yet be estimated. You will understand that I can't sleep for happiness."

One of the units that took part in this "gallop to the Egyptian frontier" was MG Battalion 8 of the 1st Panzergrenadier Regiment in 5th Leichte Division, who took over from the leading armoured reconnaissance unit (AA3) at El Agheila on 27 March. Here is a short extract from their privately published history:

"Within the battalion area are massed all the other units that are ready for the attack on the Mersa el Brega defile. Its occupation will be important for future operations, as

having to detour around all the salt lakes and salt marshes there, would take a long time especially because the terrain is completely unknown to us.

"Artillery fire is our 'Reveille' on 1 April and soon the attack is under way, although we don't move off until late morning. By about 1400 hours we are advancing on either side of the road. To our left the unit ahead of us—MG Battalion 2—has taken Mersa el Brega after having failed in the morning. The enemy directly in front of us withdraws slowly at first, but then breaks and races back, so that by dusk we are well east of Mersa el Brega on the track to Gtafia. We cannot go further as two British artillery batteries pin us down. Motorcycle patrols and Lt Wendland's platoon which has been reinforced with an anti-tank gun, recce out towards El Gtafia and Bir el Medfun, so we are kept well informed concerning the positions and movements of the enemy.

"In the early hours of the next day we drive off a British counterattack, which was

an anti-tank company and an engineer platoon, to push forward right across the desert via Giof el Matar–Bir Ben Gania–El Mechili, then on to Derna, which they were to capture. It was called Operation Ponarth after the battalion commander who led the force.

"Certainly it was an adventurous operation! Imagine it today: a journey of about 450km over completely unknown desert with vehicles designed for European road and terrain conditions, with maps that proved to be unusable, insufficient reconnaissance of the ground or of the enemy dispositions, no desert experience whatsoever—everyone from the commanding officer down to the youngest soldier was taking his life in his hands.

"The farther we travel away from the coast into the limitless desert the higher soar the daytime temperatures which, despite the time of the year, approach 50 degrees Centigrade. Shortly before last light we reach the area of Giof el Matar and there was a short halt so that everyone can get some sleep and then be briefed on the next stage. Despite the rapid onset of night—and the desert nights are dark—Oberstleutnant Ponarth continues the march, out in front of the column with his prismatic compass, while all the rest of us follow in his tracks. However, it is soon impossible to make progress in the deep, soft sand, so we have to rest and wait for the morning. At daybreak we set off once again, after pulling and pushing those vehicles that had got stuck during the night. Now at last we can recognise the soft sand and bypass it. Fortunately the going is firmer, gravelly desert, which allowed us to move at a faster speed. At around midday the column

reached a dried-up well which we reckon is Bir Bu Hagara. It seems that we are marching in right direction!

"After another six hours travelling, Ponarth's command group comes to an area which—with a great deal of imagination—could be recognised as Bir Ben Gania airfield. There, to the amazement of everyone, they find two Ju52s and between them General Rommel himself, impatiently awaiting our arrival! New orders to the commander: part of his force is to be airlifted to El Mechili, to occupy this important position. We start to load up the aircraft—but it proves to be in vain. A reconnaissance aircraft lands and reports that a force of at least 3,000 British troops occupies El Mechili. Unfortunately this 'interlude' costs us two hours before the journey can be resumed. Then, having travelled about 30km northeastwards, the column comes upon a minefield. In spite of carefully following tracks a few vehicles are damaged, which tragically results in the death and injury of several of our comrades."

Left: After the battle, a group of Afrika Korps soldiers gather around a truck—note the Nazi flag on the bonnet being used as a ground-to-air recognition signal, also the plume of oily black smoke in the background, rising from a burning tank.
(via TRH Pictures)

Below: El Agheila captured, 24 March 1941. The swastika flies over this desert stronghold for the very first time.
(Colonel T. Bock)

spearheaded by armoured cars and carriers. Then, after a short but effective artillery barrage, we carry out an attack. However, there is a minefield just in front of the British positions and they withdraw while we are breaching it. By about midday we are within 4km of Agedabia. A flank attack hits us but is parried by our 5th Company, together with No 2 Company of Panzerjäger Battalion 39. In the follow-up 17 British armoured cars and six trucks, which had got bogged down in the soft sand, were captured, together with some 30 crewmen. After a short pause the attack continues and two hours later, Agedabia is taken together with the high ground some 4.5km to its north. General Rommel sent his personal congratulations to our CO on his success.'

A few days later, they took part in a daring operation to cut off the British withdrawal route by sending a mixed force, based upon the machine gun company carrying double its usual complement of machine guns, plus

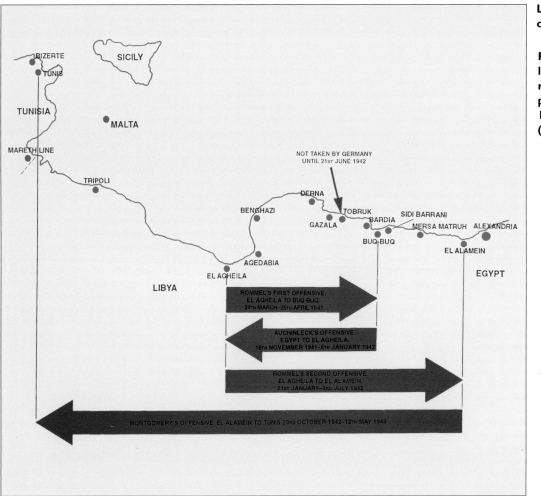

Left: The desert campaigns 1940–43.

Right: A German soldier looks for souvenirs in recently captured British positions during the May 1942 offensive. (Colonel T. Bock)

The following day, Ponarth's group was initially directed to attack El Mechili, but this was later changed and the old cry "On to Derna!" rang out. Despite the fact that they were short of everything, especially petrol, they pressed on. Part of the force was later left to block the track near Tmimi, which meant that:

"… our little force becomes smaller and smaller … At about 1600 hours we come up against the British screen. We come under artillery and tank fire. So what? We 'step on the gas' and we're through! And we do so without any casualties. With the last drop of petrol we manage to reach the area of El Ezzeiat.

"The vehicles are roughly camouflaged in a wadi, the weapons and equipment unloaded and we go forward on foot. Laden with the heavy mountings of the machine guns, with the grenade launchers and the anti-tank guns, we take up ambush positions. A British convoy is approaching at moderate speed. If only they will keep coming towards us! They continue until the leading truck is just 10 metres in front of us. It halts and we dash forward. The British officer who is dismounting stares dumbfounded into the muzzles of our rifles. Clearly he has taken us for friendly troops and perhaps our uniforms are unknown to him."

The surprised British convoy offers little resistance, so they are easily captured. Now the German column has nearly 250 prisoners and 40 trucks to look after. However, this "burden" causes great delight among "Group Ponarth", as they now have all the petrol, rations and water they need to continue their advance. Just one problem—their prisoners now exceed their own strength, and every other truck has to carry one German soldier as a guard.

"Unbroken night march as we press on. In the morning (7 April) we stop on the track to Derna. Some British fighters circle overhead. The pilots are obviously puzzled and cannot decide who has captured whom, so they don't fire at us! Soon we are only 9km from Derna. On the side of the track we intercept another column of about 100 English trucks. Leaving our captured echelon behind with a machine gun as guard, we approach the new column on a broad front. No movement, no defence—what is the reason? However, when we reach the first vehicle we learn why—the crews are all sleeping peacefully in their vehicle cabs! At first they are quite exasperated at being disturbed. It takes some time before they realise we are the enemy! They obviously hadn't expected us so far eastwards. We take another 200 prisoners. But what can we do with such a

large number? If we take them with us then our entire force will be needed just as guards. Who then will block the road? If we let them go, then in a short time we will have the British round our necks. There only remains the possibility of setting fire to their vehicles, destroying their weapons and letting them walk! This is not a question of abandoning them in the desert to die—the walk to the nearest British position we know is certainly not far. So with a friendly wave they are released. Their expressions range from astonishment to disbelief—some of them even want to stay with us! It needs emphasising with a few cries of 'Go on boys!' before they set off."

The column was now only some 3km from Derna when they met up with Oberstleutnant Ponarth's small command group, which had gone on ahead. They were leaguered in a deep gully, also looking after a large number of prisoners—another 200, including two generals, so one can imagine the excitement in both parties. Now that the force was complete again, they could go onto the offensive and capture Derna—mission accomplished!

What then was the result of Task Force Ponarth's chase across the Agedabia to Derna? The coast road at Derna had been completely blocked and 972 prisoners were taken, including four generals and 176 other

46

officers. A complete field ambulance and a field workshop were also taken, along with 240 trucks, 30 machine guns and about 400 rifles. Some 150 trucks, six transport aircraft, three carriers, two armoured cars and a tank were destroyed—and all this was accomplished by a force which had a complete lack of knowledge of the terrain or of the enemy they were facing!

By 11 April the British were back behind the Egyptian frontier wire, except for a small force of less than three brigades, holed up in Tobruk. Rommel and his "Afrikans" had gained almost mythical status, having recaptured in just half a month all the territory the British had won from the Italians. However, they were now getting dangerously far away from their bases in Tripolitania, at the end of a long, long supply line, which, despite Rommel's startling successes, made his forces considerably vulnerable. By the springtime, the 164,000-plus German and Italian troops now in North Africa required some 30 shiploads of supplies each month (about 70–80,000 tons), which far exceeded the capacity of the port of Tripoli, while the forward troops alone needed some 1,500 tons daily. This meant improving the facilities at the ports of Tripoli and Benghazi quickly and increasing the volume of supplies they received. "Rommel makes preposterous demands," commented

General Franz Halder back in Berlin, "his wishes can be satisfied only in so far as preparations for Barbarossa permit." Later on he would be even more scathing saying: "By overstepping his orders, Rommel has brought about a situation for which our present supply capabilities are insufficient." North Africa would continue to be a theatre where one side or the other was in the ascendancy one moment, advancing as fast as it could, then withdrawing the next equally speedily, when the "supply elastic" twanged it in the opposite direction!

Under pressure from Churchill to restore the situation General Wavell launched two ill-prepared counter-attacks—"Brevity" and "Battleaxe"—between May and June 1941, both of which foundered. Wavell was replaced by General Auchinleck, who was immediately under pressure to restore the situation. Both sides built up their forces between July and October 1941, then the newly established British Eighth Army launched "Crusader", which initially took the DAK by surprise, pushing it back almost level with the approaches to Tobruk. There followed the great battle of Sidi Rezegh in which both sides had mixed fortunes. However, the Germans and Italians were soon very clearly faced with a very difficult logistic situation and forced to pull back. By the end of the year they had been pushed right out of Libya and were back at their original staring point at El Agheila.

MORE OFFENSIVES AND A "BAPTISM OF FIRE"

Rommel recovered far more quickly than anyone anticipated, breaking out from El Agheila on 21 January 1942, and once again pushing the British back, first to Benghazi, then on to a defensive line running from Gazala southwards to Bir Hakeim. Both sides were by now exhausted and for four months they again built up their forces. The Germans were the first to strike. Rommel sweeping around the southern desert flank of the Gazala line, capturing the prize of Tobruk on 21 June, for which Rommel was not only awarded the Diamonds to his Knight's Cross, but also promoted to Generalfeldmarschall.

For many of his "Afrikans", this was just another campaign, but for Karl Susenberger, whose journey to Africa as a reinforcement we covered earlier, it was his "baptism of fire" as he recalled:

"*On the evening of 25 May while orders were being given out it was made known that the battalion was leaving. The tents were taken down, all the equipment stowed away and the lorries filled up. On the morning of 26 May when the battalion was ready for the off, we moved in front of the* rest of the regiment and waited for the final order to march. We didn't have long to wait. Round about noon, the powerful armada of vehicles and tanks started moving, the direction south, the name Sengali-Sud. For us common soldiers that didn't mean much, what it meant we only found out later. Towards evening the order was given to stop, but at 2100 hours we went on again and indeed travelled all that night. When it became light we had an hour's rest."

While they were halted, British recce aircraft flew over and their light flak guns managed to shoot one down. They saw that there was a big tank battle going on in front of them, with the enemy artillery "overs" landing just in front of them. It was here that Karl saw his first dead body. "We went past some knocked out tanks and stopped by a ruin. I saw a Tommy sitting in a hole, his head was laid right back, his helmet had slid from his head to one side, around him was a swarm of flies. When I got up to him I realised that he was dead. He was buried on the spot, his hidey-hole became his grave."

Moving on again, they reached Acroma on the Trigh Capuzzo and were engaged by artillery fire, which swept the whole area and continued until a sandstorm blew up. When that was over, they captured some British Bren carriers which, disorientated in the sandstorm, drove right into their column. They were next attacked by a formation of their own Stukas, which, on realising their mistake, jettisoned their bombs, but not until after hitting an 88mm flak and its towing vehicle. In the middle of this muddle, the British attacked and they had a hard time beating them back. Then, on the morning of 1 June, the battalion got ready to attack the strongpoint Got el Ulaeb, as Karl remembers:

"Shortly before the action began, radio operator Grimm and I were detailed by Lt Kordel to act as runners. As this was our first action, we were mighty scared. Who hasn't felt this way before his first action? Our preparations took place in the basin of the Trigh Capuzzo so that the enemy could not see us. The attack was scheduled to begin at 0715 hours; perched on the vehicles we waited. I had my machine pistol with three replacement magazines on its sling. I was in low spirits with all sorts of confused thoughts going through my head. I thought hopefully 'you'll make it, you won't die at only 19.' I looked over at Grimm, and it was obvious he felt the same way. All at once our Stukas came over and their bombs fell right on the English stronghold. Scarcely had they let the last bombs fall than everything started to fire and an immense wall of dust loomed up in front of us, blocking Tommy's vision. We

were able to get within 600 metres of the strongpoint before the defensive fire began. Now we got out of our vehicles and moved forward in an extended line. We tried to get nearer to the English by moving in bounds. Their defensive fire got fiercer and the first of the wounded began to call for the medics. It became increasingly difficult to get forward, especially as we could see practically nothing of their front line. I remained close to Lt Kordel so as to be on hand quickly. Crouching, jumping and running in zigzags, we reached the first English barbed wire. I had taken cover behind a camel thorn bush and was bathed in sweat, my throat was so dry that I took a hefty swig out of my water bottle. The

engineers were there and in spite of the murderous defensive fire, they had to clear a path through the minefield so that we could get through safely. The lads were superb, they managed it OK. Our heavy weapons, artillery, anti-tank and SS flak carpeted the English positions. About 0900 hours we succeeded in breaking in.

"From the forward positions we took between 90 and 100 prisoners, but it wasn't over yet. Lt Kordel called to me: 'Susenberger come with me, we'll bring the 20mm forward.' We both dashed away and succeeded in getting it up to the point at which we had broken in. From behind, the artillery and SSs boomed even deeper into the strongpoint. By midday we had taken a

arge portion of the British positions. The prisoners had increased in numbers and Grimm and I received the order to take them to the rear. More and more came out of the depths so we had to make the journey several times. Towards 1600 hours the stronghold fell and we counted 1,800 prisoners. Eight of us had just taken them back to division, which lay about three kilometres behind. This was a hard bit of work because the column kept getting split up and we had to watch them very closely. After handing them over at division, our driver Bernd Ray took us back to the stronghold. We saw now the havoc wreaked by our heavy weapons; dead lay everywhere, burnt out tanks, lorries, guns etc.

"On the journey back to the battalion we saw an English tent in a small depression. Bernd drove right up to see what was happening. With machine pistols at the ready, we went up to the tent and fetched out of it the Tommies, who were hiding there. We disarmed them, but had to take them back to battalion on foot as they wouldn't fit into the car. When we arrived we reported to Lt Kordel, who said 'Where on earth did you find them?' Bernd told him and on Kordel's orders we took them back to division.

"I came out of my baptism of fire fairly well I think, slightly bashed, but it was endurable. We then set out to march on the Trigh Capuzzo in regimental and divisional formation."

Top: Convoys of DAK vehicles usually kept to the coast road as this one is doing. (*Rolf Munninger*)

Above: Often moving ahead of his leading troops, the "Desert Fox," made considerable use of the Fieseler Fi156 *Storch* (Stork) light reconnaissance/army co-operation aircraft, which could both land and take-off in very confined spaces. (*Rolf Munninger*)

Above Left: More work for the regimental cobbler! *Der Schusterei* was always busy, even in the desert. (*via TRH Pictures*)

ON TO ALAM HALFA

Following the capture of Tobruk, the Axis forces continued to push their British and Commonwealth opponents steadily back to a defensive line from El Alamein to the Qattara Depression. It must have appeared that there was now nothing to prevent Rommel pushing on deep into Egypt, capturing Cairo, Alexandria, even the Suez Canal. However, the British were equally determined that they would not allow this to happen. The charismatic new Eighth Army Commander, Lieutenant General Bernard Montgomery, issued the first of his famous "Orders of the Day" to his men: "We will fight the enemy where we now stand: there will be no withdrawal and no surrender. Every officer and man must continue to do his duty as long as he has breath in his body."

This would be the limit of the DAK's successes. Having fought its way forwards and backwards and then forwards again, with its morale at an all time high, the tide of battle was about to turn against it .

Top: DAK infantry attacking in extended order, as they approach the Egyptian border. (*Colonel T. Bock*)

Above: British and Indian prisoners on their way to POW camp. Note the metal sand channels on the side of the vehicle—essential for negotiating soft sand. (Rolf Munninger)

Right: An MG34 light machine gun crew comes into action, somewhere in North Africa, while a third man spots for them. Note also the bivouac tent to the rear. (*via TRH Pictures*)

Chapter 5 Into Russia

OPERATION BARBAROSSA

"And so we National Socialists consciously draw a line beneath the foreign policy tendency of our prewar period. We take up where we broke off six hundred years ago. We stop the endless German movement to the south and west, and turn our gaze towards the land in the east … If we speak of soil in Europe today, we can primarily have in mind only Russia and her vassal border states."

Adolf Hitler, writing in *Mein Kampf*

It was the Führer's insatiable desire for more and more *Lebensraum* (living space), which was at the root of his decision to turn on his erstwhile ally, the Soviet Union, despite dissent from some senior German officers, like Panzer general, Heinz Guderian, who said, after the plan had been explained to him on a large-scale map of Russia: "I could scarcely believe my eyes … Was something which I had held to be utterly impossible now to become fact? … I made no attempt to conceal my disappointment and disgust." He was not alone.

However, he might as well have saved his breath, because his Führer would brook no argument, and so it came to pass that, at 0315 hours on 22 June 1941, three massive German army groups—North (26 divisions under von Leeb), Centre (51 divisions under von Bock) and South (59 divisions under von Rundstedt), each headed by a Panzer group, attacked on a 2,000-mile front from Memel on the Baltic to the Black Sea. Everywhere the Russian divisions under Voroshilov, Timoshenko and Budenny were pushed back in considerable disorder. And so it continued. By the autumn, the Germans had advanced some 550 miles, occupying 500,000 square miles of Soviet territory, inflicting 2.5 million casualties on the Red Army and taking over a million prisoners. However, despite this crushing defeat, key, heavily-defended cities like Leningrad did not fall, while the Soviets operated a scorched earth policy, allowing the bitter winter weather that followed to take its savage toll of the German Army.

Above: **Convoys of vehicles and weapons move up towards the Russian frontier.** (*E. Moog*)

Left: **The troops wait for the "off", doing all the things one would expect them to do like eating, writing letters home, etc.** (*E. Moog*)

Right: **German infantry on the march in Russia. Despite the much-heralded mechanised Blitzkrieg tactics, most of the German infantry still had to march into battle. (*via TRH Pictures*)**

Below: **River crossing as "Barbarossa" begins.** (*E. Moog*)

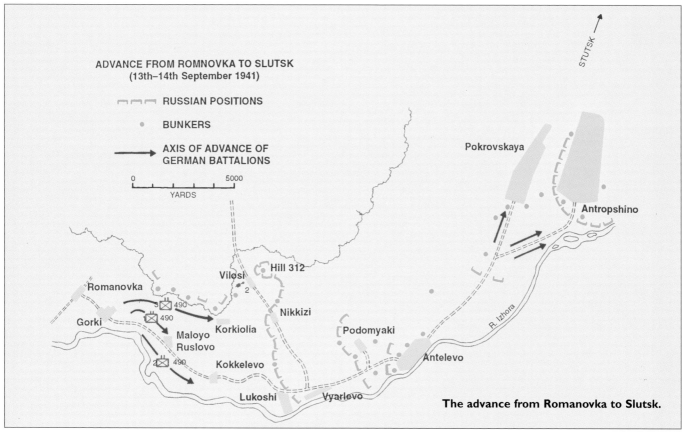

ADVANCE FROM ROMNOVKA TO SLUTSK
(13th–14th September 1941)

⊓⊓⊓ RUSSIAN POSITIONS

• BUNKERS

→ AXIS OF ADVANCE OF
GERMAN BATTALIONS

0 ——————————— 5000
YARDS

STUTSK →

Pokrovskaya

Antropshino

Vilosi   Hill 312

Romanovka

Nikkizi

Gorki

Korkiolia

Maloyo
Ruslovo

Podomyaki

Kokkelevo

Antelevo

R. Izhora

Lukoshi   Vyarlevo

The advance from Romanovka to Slutsk.

A TYPICAL EARLY ACTION

During the late summer, while the Germans
were slowly forging a "ring of steel" around
Leningrad, 490th Infantry Regiment was
given the mission of eliminating enemy
centres of resistance some 15 miles south of
the city in the area north of the River
Izhora, between Romanovka and Slutsk. In
this area were numerous Red Army bunkers
and defensive positions, located in the hills
that dominated the river valley. It was these
positions which had to be neutralised by the
490th so as to secure the German lines of
communication. Late on 13 September, the
regiment crossed the river, south of Gorki
(see sketch-map above) and spent the night
in the village.

The attack against the Russian-held
hills would start the next day, with the 1st
and 2nd Battalions advancing along the
river valley, while the 3rd Battalion
provided flank protection to the north. The
regiment had very little information about
the general area and the enemy locations.
This was because the maps they were
using—captured previously from the
enemy—were both inadequate and
inaccurate. Therefore, the commander of
the 3rd Battalion decided to carry out a
careful reconnaissance of the terrain before
attacking. This took the entire morning, so
the attack did not begin until noon. Using
flamethrowers and shaped charges, German
engineer demolition teams went to work,

Right and Below: The advance into Russia was rapid with a great deal of what would be called "collateral damage" in a later war. With no regard for the civilian population, and the *Einsatzgruppen* awaiting their chance to perform "ethnic cleansing" behind them, the good weather, Russian unpreparedness, and German skill at arms saw great encircling battles fought and hundreds of thousands of Russians captured in the summer of 1942—up to one and a half million at Kiev and Uman in the Ukraine. These photographs show burning buildings and bemused peasants. (E. Moog)

moving ahead of the infantry, but were interrupted by enemy howitzer fire. Fortunately, the regimental artillery quickly destroyed the howitzers and a nearby ammunition dump. Nevertheless, although the demolition teams were successful, it was a slow business as they advanced towards Hill 312. By late afternoon on the 14th, they had made some gains, but halted after last light and withdrew to the village of Vilosi for the night. The other two battalions had made only a little headway and they spent the night at the eastern edge of Vyarlevo. Taking up the narrative (as reported in a US Army historical study of July 1953):

"The seizure of strongly fortified Hill 312, scheduled for the next day, promised to be an arduous task. Although H-hour had originally been set for 0600 hours, the attack had to be postponed until the afternoon, because the morning hours were needed for a thorough terrain reconnaissance by two patrols sent out by 3rd Battalion.

"One of these patrols, led by Lt Thomsen, was to reconnoitre the hills between Korkiolia and Lukashi to determine whether and in what strength they were occupied by the Russians. The second patrol, under Sgt Ewald, was to reconnoitre the area north of Hill 312, to determine the enemy's dispositions and strength, and to probe for weak spots in his defence.

"Patrol Thomsen was stealthily advancing southeastwards from Korkiolia when it was suddenly intercepted and pinned down. In the ensuing exchange of fire the patrol was able to identify a number of Russian bunkers and field positions and to relay the necessary target information to the 3rd Battalion CP. A short time later the accurate fire of the regimental artillery destroyed these Russian strongpoints. After having completed their mission, Patrol Thomsen returned to battalion headquarters.

"By noon no word from Patrol Ewald had been received by the commander of the 3rd Battalion. Since he could not postpone the attack on Hill 312 any longer, he ordered Lt Hahn, the commander of Company I, to seize the hill."

At 1230 hours Hahn assembled the assault force, which consisted of Company I plus a machine gun platoon and a mortar platoon, a demolition team consisting of two engineers equipped with flamethrowers and shaped charges, and an artillery observer. Since Sgt Ewald's patrol had still not returned, only the two platoons led by Lt Borgwardt and Sgt Timm were available for the attack. In extended formation, the assault force advanced through the woods west and northwest of Vilosi and reached a point north of Hill 312 apparently without attracting the enemy's attention. From there, Lt Hahn identified the bunker on top of Hill 312 and two positions on its northern slope

The fortifications were held in strength. Before he was able to finish his observations. the enemy spotted the Germans. fired on them and pinned them down.

"The artillery observer attached to the assault force called for direct howitzer fire, whereupon the bunker received two direct hits which appeared to do little damage. Hahn reported the situation to battalion headquarters and was ordered to continue the attack.

"Platoons Borgwardt and Timm were to skirt Hill 312 and approach its base through the dense thicket that extended southward from the forest edge to the hill. Platoon Borgwardt went to the right, Platoon Timm to the left. The latter was to support Borgwardt's advance up the hill and then dispose of the obstinate bunker on the crest of the hill as soon as Borgwardt had entered the two slope positions. While the two platoons were moving out, the attached machine gun and mortar platoons went into position at the edge of the forest north of Hill 312. The howitzers gave the signal to attack by firing six rounds at the enemy bunker on top of Hill 312. Company HQ personnel had to act as a covering force since an enemy relief thrust was expected at any time."

Again the fire of the howitzers failed to put the bunker out of action. While the shells were exploding on and around the bunker.

Borgwardt's men stealthily worked their way up the hill. creeping towards the two Russian positions whose occupants' attention was diverted by machine gun and mortar fire from the edge of the woods north of the hill. Platoon Borgwardt suddenly broke into the positions and caught the Russians completely by surprise.

"While Borgwardt's men were engaged in seizing the two positions, Platoon Timm followed them up the hill and captured the bunker with the help of the engineers, whose flamethrowers and shaped charges

Above: Camouflaged to blend in with their cornfield background, a light flak guncrew goes into action. (*via TRH Pictures*)

Below: The German infantry moves on deeper and deeper into Russia. (E. Moog)

Above, Right, and Far Right: It is easy to forget that Blitzkrieg—"Lightning War"—with all its connotations of speed, mechanisation and modernity was all very well when the logistic distances were short, as they were in Poland and the west, but the sheer size of Russia, the speed of the advance, and—after October—the effects of the weather all degraded German mechanised transportation.

As the dusty roads of summer turned to the churned mud of autumn, and then gave way to "General Winter", with temperatures down to -40°C, the German Army found itself little better off than Napoleon in the century before. By the end of the war, it is said, there were more horses than men in the German Army. (This Page— E. Moog; Opposite—via TRH Pictures)

Right: The German casualty levels rose steadily during 1942 as the veterans of the early campaigns, particularly the backbone of the army, the junior officers and NCOs, died. Here an honour guard stands over 11 more graves, their occupants' steel helmets used as grave markers. (E. Moog)

succeeded where the artillery had failed. Just as the operation seemed to have been brought to a successful conclusion, the personnel who had remained at the edge of the forest north of Hill 312 were attacked from behind by a force of about 50 Russians. Hahn ordered the newly arrived Patrol Ewald to hold off the Russians while the rest of the assault force followed the elements that had captured the hill. Upon arriving at the summit they immediately set up their weapons, took the Russians under effective fire and repulsed their attack. From the top of the hill, Hahn saw the 1st Battalion, now no longer subject to flanking fire from Hill 312, penetrate the Russian positions west of Nikkizi. He immediately established contact with the battalion commander and made preparations to defend the hill against a potential Russian counterattack. This precaution proved to be very sensible, for within the hour the artillery observer on the top of the hill, noticed Russian forces assembling for a counterattack in the woods north and northeast of Hill 312. However, the Russians lost all enthusiasm for the attack after the German artillery lobbed a few well-aimed shells into their midst.

"After the capture of the hill on the afternoon of the 15th, the 3rd Battalion continued its advance on the left of the 490th Infantry Regiment. Russian resistance was light and the battalion had little difficulty in occupying Podomyaki since the Russians had evacuated the fortified position west of the village and had withdrawn to Antelevo.

"On the morning of 17 September the 3rd Battalion prepared to advance from the northwest towards Antelevo, which the Russians appeared to be defending in strength. The Russian positions west and north of the village were situated on high ground dominating terrain over which the battalion had to advance; to the south and east Antelevo was protected by the River Izora. At dawn a reconnaissance patrol from Company 1 identified two concrete bunkers as well as field emplacements in and around Antelevo. A Russian battalion held the northern and western sectors of the village. German howitzers and anti-tank guns took the bunkers under fire, though only with little effect. Once again demolition teams were needed to destroy the enemy fortifications with shaped charges. The flamethrowers, which previously had proved so effective, could no longer be used since the supply of flamethrower fuel had been exhausted.

"By an unexpected stroke of luck, the recce patrol managed to capture a Russian outpost whose telephone was still connected to the CP of the Russian commander at Antelevo. The German battalion commander immediately interrogated the captured Russian telephone operator and obtained the latter's code name. His next step was to put his knowledge of Russian to the test. Using the code name of the Russian telephone operator he called the Russian regimental commander. The latter was apparently misled, but did not divulge anything of value except that he was determined to hold Antelevo. When the German officer became more insistent in his quest for additional information, the suspicions of the Russian commander were aroused, and he changed his tone. The German tried a more direct approach and made an outright demand for the surrender of the Russian regiment at Antelevo. This was curtly rejected.

"The commander of the 490th thereupon decided to mass his forces and seize Antelevo by direct assault. During the afternoon of the 17th he assembled the 1st and 3rd Battalions west and north of the village, respectively, and launched an attack on the enemy stronghold after strong artillery preparation. Again the demolition teams performed their task in an exemplary manner and quickly put one Russian bunker after another out of action. The Russians had apparently considered these particular bunkers impregnable, for once they had been destroyed the infantry fled in wild disorder, abandoning their equipment. By nightfall Antelevo was in German hands.

"With the fall of Antelevo Russian resistance seemed to disintegrate all along the regiment's route of advance, except for a brief encounter at the road fork south of Antropshino. There the Russians attempted to stop the regiment along prepared positions, but failed to do so. After this delay, the German forces fanned out and reached Slutsk on 18 September, the 3rd Battalion via Pokrovskaya and the 1st and 2nd via Antropshino. Upon its arrival in Slutsk the regiment established contact with the 121st Infantry Division, which had previously captured the town.

"A number of lessons may be learnt from this operation. First, all regimental units had to conduct thorough terrain reconnaissance since their maps and those captured from the Russians were frequently either inadequate or inaccurate. Whenever one of the battalion commanders failed to reconnoitre the terrain thoroughly, his unit was in danger of being ambushed by the Russians. The Germans were able to take the Russian bunkers with a minimum loss of time and men by employing skilled demolition teams. Each member of these teams had been thoroughly trained and was well versed in his task. The capture of the Russian outpost on the morning of 17 September might have provided the Germans with information about the Russian intentions and troop dispositions if it had been properly exploited. The battalion commander showed a lack of good judgement by using his average knowledge of Russian in an attempt to extract information from the Russian regimental commander. This was clearly a task for an expert interpreter who was skilled in methods of interrogation.

"The Russians were fighting a delaying action during which they often failed to take advantage of the favourable terrain and of their prepared positions. The flight of the Antelevo garrison was indicative of how easily the Russians became demoralised when they were confronted by an unexpected situation. When the German demolition teams blew up the bunkers with shaped charges, the Russians panicked and instinctively took to flight, as happened so often during the early months of the campaign."

Above Right: Summertime in Russia. "Barbarossa" went so well in the summer sunshine and the Germans were supremely confident of an easy victory. The vast steppes and harsh Russian winter would soon shake their optimism. (*via TRH Pictures*)

Right: There were few chances for a rest during the advance and, as the Soviet scorched earth policy took hold, so did the German dependence on horse-drawn logistic and supply wagons. (E. Moog)

FIGHTING IN A RUSSIAN WINTER

As the weather deteriorated in the late autumn and early winter of 1941, Red Army resistance began to stiffen, especially as the Germans got closer to Moscow—by 30 October they were only some 45–75 miles from the city's outer defences, but were delayed by the heavy rains, followed swiftly by the first snows of the winter. Neither side was particularly well equipped with winter clothing during that first winter. Many, especially on the Russian side, were still dressed in their thin summer uniforms. They also seemed to have been just as susceptible to cold as the Germans and used to issue tablets (five per man), which had a similar effect to that of alcohol, plus a large ration of sugar cubes. Together they were supposed to counteract the discomfort caused by the low temperatures and freezing conditions! For the Germans the ever-lengthening lines of supply compounded their difficulties as did the unending snow, which simply got deeper and deeper. The problems that the deep snow caused are admirably described in another small unit action entitled *Company G operates in deep snow* (January 1942).

"On 13 January, Company G of the 464th Infantry Regiment was ordered to provide protection against Russian partisan raids on the division's supply line, which led from Toroprets via Village M (see map) to Village O. To this end the company was reinforced by two heavy machine guns, two 8cm mortars and one anti-tank platoon.

"On the evening of 14 January, the company, mounted in trucks, reached Village O, five miles east of Village M. Upon its arrival, a supply unit which was fleeing westwards towards Rzhev before the powerful Russian offensive, indicated that strong contingents of Russian troops from the north had cut the German supply route in the forest west of Village N. Using civilian labour the Russians had constructed a road at least 30 miles long that led south through the large forest, bypassing Toropets to the east. The Company commander, Lt. Viehmann, decided to establish local security in Village O, spend the night there and continue westwards on foot the following morning, in order to see what was going on. During the night a few Russian civilians slipped out of the village, established contact with the Russian troops and supplied them with intelligence regarding the German dispositions.

"At dawn on 15 January, after posting security details, the company started out and arrived at Village M without having made any contact with the Russians. As the company's advance element approached Village N, the Germans noticed a large group of soldiers in German uniform standing in the road, beckoning to them. That these soldiers were not Germans became evident when the anti tank gun, moving up behind the advance element was suddenly fired upon. The company's other anti tank guns covered the advance elements withdrawal to Village M, where it rejoined the main body of the company. The prime mover of the lead gun was lost during this action. The Russians, however, did not follow up their attack.

"In Village M the company set up hasty defences against an attack from the north and west and tried to determine the strength and intentions of the opposing Russian force. From a vantage point in the village it was possible to observe the eastern edge of Village N, where the Russians were building snow positions and moving four anti tank guns into position. There was an exchange of fire but no indication of an impending Russian attack. During the hours of darkness Company G built snow positions along the western and northern

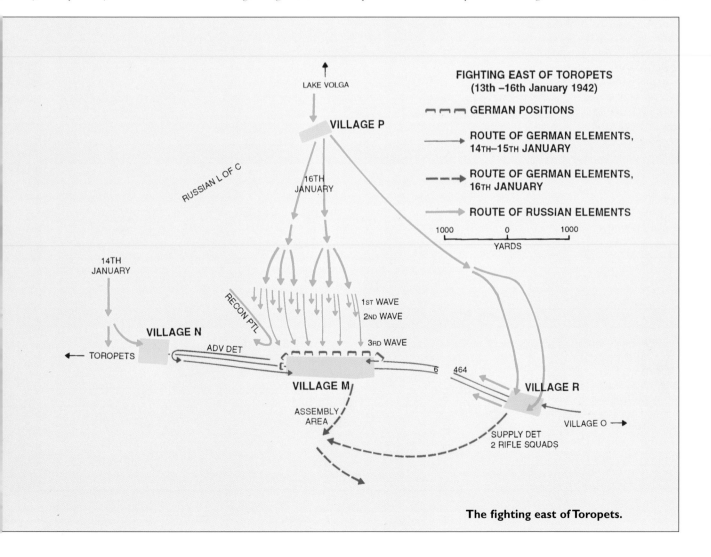

The fighting east of Toropets.

Above: The original caption to this photograph reads: "150 kilometres to Moscow"—but the winter was coming. Operation Typhoon took German troops to the outskirts of the city, close enough to see the spires, but the arrival of Russian General Georgi Zhukov and a 6 December counterattack knocked the cup from the German lips. They would not get a second chance. (E. Moog)

edges of Village M, while the aforementioned supply unit occupied Village R, about a mile east of Village M, and took measures to secure it, particularly from the north.

"During the night of 15–16 January reconnaissance patrols reported that the Russians were continuing their defensive preparations in Village N and that their line of communications was the road leading north from there.

"On 16 January between 0400 and 0600 hours, a 50-man Russian reconnaissance patrol approached the northwest corner of Village M on skis. Although the Russian patrol had been detected, it was allowed to come very close before it was fired upon. Approximately ten of the patrol escaped and three were taken prisoner, the rest were killed before they could reach the German position. According to the statements of the three prisoners, two Russian divisions were moving south towards Village M. On 16 January, Villages M and R were to be captured. What the prisoners either did not know or refused to tell, was that the Russians, attacking in force across the frozen Lake Volga, had broken through the German positions west of the 253rd Infantry Division two days before and had pushed on to the south. Thus Viehmann was unaware of the true German situation.

"Since the Russians in Village N remained passive, Viehmann decided to concentrate on defending his village against

an attack from the north. The deep snow caused some difficulties; for instance, machine guns had to be mounted on anti-aircraft tripods so that a satisfactory field of fire could be obtained.

"About 0800 hours on 16 January the company's observation post identified three Russian columns moving south towards the forest north of Village M. Except for anti-tank guns these columns did not seem to be equipped with heavy weapons. Around 1000 hours the first Russian appeared on the southern end of the forest, some 1,000 yards from the German defensive positions. At 1020 hours the Russian centre and right-wing columns attacked with anti-tank guns and infantry. Just a short time before this attack Company G had dispatched two rifle squads to Village R to reinforce the supply unit there, since the Russian left-wing column was heading in that direction.

"The first wave of Russian infantry, some 400 men strong, emerged from the forest on a broad front. It was evident that the three foot snow was causing them great difficulty. The concentrated fire of the German heavy weapons succeeded in halting the attack after it had advanced about 200 yards. After a short while a second, equally large wave emerged from the forest. It advanced in the tracks of the first and carried the attack over and beyond the line of the dead. The Russian anti-tank fire became heavier, directed against the German machine gun positions.

Above: In autumn and winter freezing conditions and full snow were often better for movement than the muddy slush that followed. (E. Moog)

which the Russians had spotted. As a result, several machine guns were destroyed; some changed position frequently in an effort to dodge the Russian fire. The Russians advanced an additional 200 yards, then bogged down under the effective German small arms fire. They sustained heavy losses, which, however, were compensated for by the reinforcements pouring down south into the forest from Village P. Viehmann estimated that the Russians committed the equivalent of two regiments in this action.

"By 1100 hours the Russian left-wing column had reached a point 150 yards from the German positions in Village R, where the terrain was more favourable for the attacker than that north of Village M. The supply unit and the two rifle squads defending Village R could no longer be reinforced because the road from Village M was under constant Russian fire.

"Realising that his position would become untenable within the next few hours, Viehmann ordered his men to prepare to evacuate Village M. A few men with minor wounds were detailed to trample a path through the deep snow from Village M towards the forest to the south in order to facilitate a quick withdrawal. The troops in Village R were also to withdraw to the same forest if pressed too heavily by the Russians.

"The members of the third Russian assault wave emerged from the forest unarmed. However, they armed themselves quickly with the weapons of their fallen comrades and continued the attack. Meanwhile, Village R was taken and the Russian closed on Village M from the east. The Germans were now very low on ammunition, having expended almost 20,000 rounds during the fighting.

"About 1300 hours Company G, after destroying its mortars and anti-tank guns, evacuated Village M. Viehmann planned to make contact with the German troops in Village O by withdrawing through the forest south of Village M. He ordered the evacuation of the wounded, then withdrew with the main body of the company and left behind a light machine gun and an anti-tank gun to provide covering fire and to simulate a larger force. After the gun crews had expended all their ammunition, they destroyed the breech operating mechanism of the anti-tank gun and withdrew into the forest. About halfway there they were fired on by the Russians who had entered Village M. The retreating Germans managed to escape without loss because the Russians did not pursue them into the forest.

"During the next three days the company marched—with almost no halts for rest—through the deep snow which blanketed the dense forest, relying heavily on a compass in absence of familiar landmarks. On 19 January, after bypassing Village O, which was found to be occupied by the Russians, it finally re-established contact with the 253rd Infantry Division. Only then did the company learn that all forces on the German front south of and

STALEMATE

As 1941 ended both sides had been forced into inactivity by the appalling weather and so 1942 opened with German forces deployed all along the front from the Crimea in the south to Finland in the north, in a series of large defensive camps known as "hedgehogs". It was now the Red Army's turn to launch a series of winter counter-offensives, which, although they enjoyed considerable local success, were not sufficiently well co-ordinated to produce lasting advantages.

In March, the mud of the spring thaw again caused problems, but there was still a great deal of action in which the Germans had to deal with overwhelming enemy odds. Typical is this action in which a Russian infantry regiment endeavoured to cut off some German units and link up with friendly forces moving in from the opposite direction. Again it is one of the "Small Unit Actions" covered in the US Army pamphlet No 20-269, under the title: *Company G struggles against overwhelming odds* (March 1942).

"The following action shows a Russian regiment attacking eastward in an attempt to cut off some German units and link up with friendly forces moving in from the opposite direction. The attack methods employed by the Russian infantry showed that the troops were inadequately trained. The infantry emerged from their jump off position in a disorderly manner, having the appearance of a disorganised herd that suddenly emerged from a forest. As soon as the Germans opened fire, panic developed in the ranks of the attack force. The infantrymen had to be driven forward by three or four officers with drawn pistols. In many instances any attempt to retreat or even to glance backwards was punished by immediate execution. There was virtually no fire support or coordinated fire.

"Typical of Russian infantry tactics was the tenacity with which the attack was repeated over and over again. The Russians never abandoned ground that they had gained in an attack. Frequently, isolated Russian soldiers would feign death, only to surprise approaching Germans by suddenly coming to life and firing at them from close range.

"In February 1942, the 2nd Battalion of the 464th German Infantry Regiment occupied snow positions without bunkers or dugouts along the western edge of Village T, situated north of Olenino near the rail line leading from Rzhev to Velikiye Luki [see map]. German reconnaissance patrols probing through the forest west of the village had been unable to establish contact with the Russians. Towards the end of February, a reconnaissance patrol

Above: Flak mountings for machine guns often had to be used just to get the weapon above the height of the deep snow. (E. Moog)

Above Right: The defence of village T.

parallel to Lake Volga had been withdrawn in the meantime.

"In this action deep snow hampered the movements of both the attacking Russians and the defending Germans. Only by trampling a path before it withdrew from Village M did Company G avoid being trapped by the Russians. The appearance of a Russian recce patrol in German uniform was a frequent occurrence; however, the number of disguised Russians encountered on 15 January in Village N was unusually large.

"As so often happened during the winter of 1941–42, the Russians attacked in several waves on a given front, each successive wave passing over the dead of the preceding wave and carrying the attack forward to a point where it, too, was destroyed. Some waves started out unarmed and recovered the weapons from their fallen comrades."

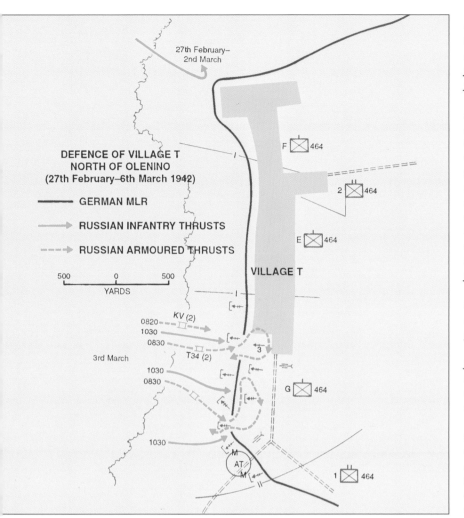

DEFENCE OF VILLAGE T
NORTH OF OLENINO
(27th February–6th March 1942)

━━━━ GERMAN MLR

➜ RUSSIAN INFANTRY THRUSTS

⇢ RUSSIAN ARMOURED THRUSTS

500   0   500
YARDS

VILLAGE T

KV (2)

T34 (2)

3rd March

ascertained the presence of Russian forces in the forest. Subsequent information obtained from local inhabitants indicated that the Russians were being reinforced for an attack.

"From 27 February to 2 March, detachments, consisting of about 80 Russians each, attacked daily in the same sector and at the same time. The attacks took place about an hour after sunrise and were directed against a point at the northwest edge of Village T. Every one of them was unsuccessful, the attacking Russians being wiped out before they could reach the German position.

"On the evening of 2 March a Russian deserter reported that his infantry regiment, supported by six tanks, would attack Company G's sector which was south of the village. To strengthen this sector, the company commander, Lt Viehmann, placed three 37mm anti tank guns behind the Main Line of Resistance (MLR) and planted anti-tank mines across the road leading southwestwards. Although his unit was understrength, Viehmann ordered each platoon to form a reserve detachment of ten men for a possible counterthrust.

"At daybreak on 3 March, two Russian heavy tanks of their KV type, painted white to blend with the landscape, were spotted

standing at the edge of the forest about 500 yards in front of Company G's sector. At 0820 hours, Russian aircraft bombed the village, while the two tanks, about 150 yards apart, advanced another 100 yards, stopped, and opened fire at the most conspicuous German fortifications. At 0830 hours, four more Russian tanks, this time T-34s, emerged from the forest. They paired off, penetrated the right and centre of Company G's MLR and rolled up the stretch between the two points of penetration. Encountering no effective resistance, they pushed deeper into the German defensive position while providing mutual fire support. The three German 37mm anti-tank guns proved ineffective against the T-34s and were quickly knocked out as were a number of German heavy weapons. However, without immediate infantry support, the Russian tanks were incapable of achieving any further results

"It was not until two hours later that approximately 300 Russian riflemen attacked from the forest, while the two KV tanks stood still and the T-34s roamed at will through the depth of the German position. Hampered by the deep snow, the infantry had to bunch up and advance along the tank tracks, offering easy targets due to their slow movement. Despite the loss

of many of their heavy weapons, the German defenders mustered sufficient strength to repel the Russian attack and to force the infantry to withdraw into the forest, the tanks following soon afterwards.

"A short time later the four T-34s reappeared. This time each tank carried a rifle squad. Additional infantry supported the attack. When the T-34s re-entered the German MLR, three of them were eliminated by German infantrymen who threw anti-tank mines into their paths. The Russian foot infantry elements then advanced 350 yards from the forest edge before being pinned down by German mortar fire. The one tank that remained intact quickly withdrew into the forest, followed by the Russian infantry. Throughout the day the two KVs remained in the German position and fired at anything that moved within the German position.

"Russian prisoners taken during the fighting said that the riflemen mounted on the tanks had been ordered to establish themselves within the German position, so as to support the dismounted infantry's attack. These statements were confirmed when it was discovered that a small number of Russian detachments had infiltrated the German outpost area, from where they refused to be dislodged despite the severe cold. After dark, German combat patrols were finally able to move out and liquidate them.

"All was quiet on 4 March. The next day the Russians resumed their attack all along the 2nd Battalion sector with a force estimated at two to three infantry regiments and supported by 16 tanks. While the Russian artillery confined itself to harassing the German rear area, the mortars laid down intensive fire, whose effect was insignificant because of the deep snow. Severe fighting continued unabated until evening. After dark the Russians broke into the southern part of Village T at several points. By that time severe losses in men and matériel had greatly weakened the defending forces. Nevertheless, the Germans held the northern part of Village T, until the morning of 6 March, when they withdrew to a new position two miles farther east.

"The Russian troops employed in this action seemed to be particularly immune to extreme cold—for example, individual snipers hid in deep snow throughout the day or night at temperatures as low as –50°F. In temperatures of –40°F and below, the German machine guns often failed to function and below –60°F some of the rifles failed to fire. In these temperatures the oil and grease congealed, jamming the bolt mechanism. Locally produced sunflower oil was used as a lubricant when available, as it guaranteed the proper functioning of weapons in sub-zero temperatures."

Chapter 6 Battlefield Living

I f a soldier is to survive on a battlefield, then he must learn many skills in addition to those which make him master of his weapons and equipment. He must also become the master of his environment, able to conceal himself from ground and air, able to move across any type of terrain and to live under any climatic conditions from the baking deserts of North Africa to freezing steppes of Russia. Normal acts like what to wear, how to feed oneself, how to wash and keep free from bugs and infection—even how to defecate!—could cause problems every bit as serious as wounds received in battle if neglected. The photographs in this section show soldiers coping with a wide range of these activities, from eating to delousing, or from keeping cool to preventing frostbite.

THE "STAFF OF LIFE"

German rations were spartan—and always included such staple items as ersatz coffee and black bread. The food was generally cooked in bulk in horse-drawn (two or four horses dependent on the size) field kitchens, then brought forward in containers for distribution in the front line. For all ranks, from officers down to private soldiers, the food from the field kitchens was the same—adequate but monotonous. It was wonderful when one had a break in reserve and could cook more varied food, or—because the "grass was always greener on the other side of the fence"—when it was possible to dine off captured enemy supplies. Hubert Gees, recalled his days in Holland in September 1944:

"It is an inexplicable secret just how the smoking field kitchen turns up when it's needed. How often had I sworn about Hauptfeldwebel Wigl and damned him as a pig and a shirker, but when things got really fiery he was always there at the right time. 'We've got coffee and dried vegetables and there's a bottle of wine for every four men.'

"'You're a marvel! better start getting it dished out at once because we don't know what will happen in the next half hour.'"

"I remember how we bought a calf from the owner of this house. We collected the money for it from among our soldiers. I
think it was occupation money and it probably wasn't worth much any more but we didn't have anything else. We also gave him a receipt that we had bought the calf from him. Amongst our men were two butchers and they took care of the calf. The Dutch women cooked the meat and prepared the evening dinner. They received the rest of the meat.

"The next day our group of soldiers left and we marched in a long column through the city of Maastricht, a beautiful city with its wonderful chimes. I was already impressed by the nice and clean houses of the Dutch. Their houses didn't have curtains like our houses and you could see their nicely furnished living rooms from outside in the street."

Top and Above: "Come to the cookhouse door boys!" Whatever the conditions, soldiers had to be fed. (Author's collection and Erich Moog)

Right: A group of soldiers eating from their mess tins. All ranks in a German infantry unit ate exactly the same food. (via TRH Pictures)

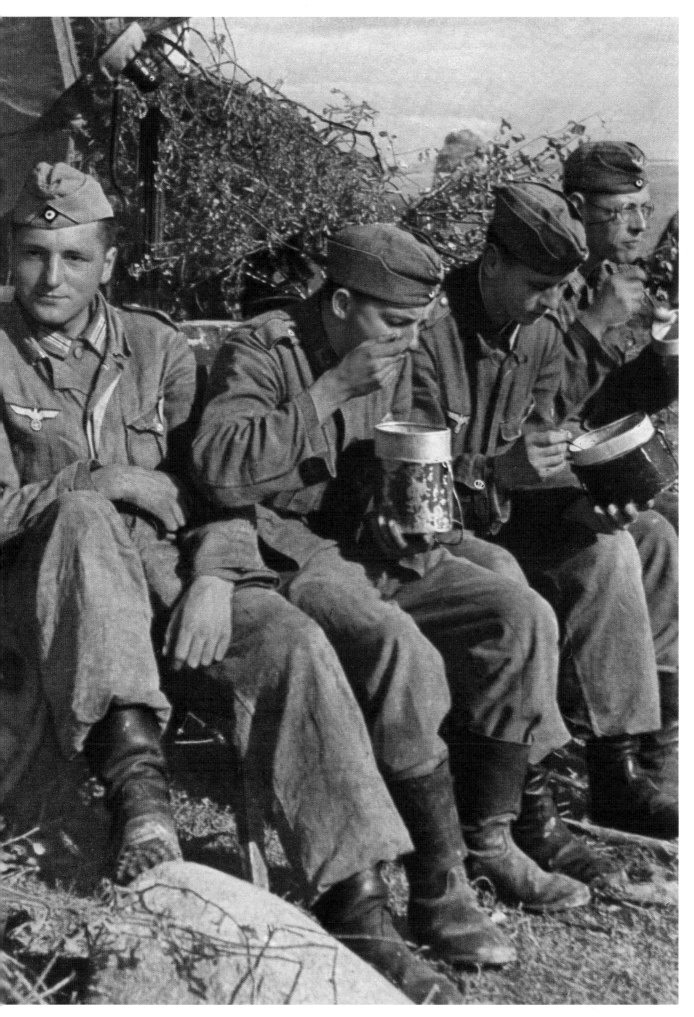

Otto Gunkel recalled:

"During the night of 15 January 1945, I had an experience that I still recall as one of the most impressive and beautiful of my time as a soldier. Sgt Holler and myself had to take some much-needed supplies to a unit at Herhan. A sledge, drawn by two horses, awaited us at the Ruhr River dam. We covered ourselves in blankets and we had a ride for several hours through a wonderful, moonlit winter landscape, alongside the dam lake. It was a winter fairy tale and I could almost forget about the war. However, as I tried a sudden salvo of incoming artillery shells brought me back to deadly reality."

"YOU'LL DO YOUR WORK ON WATER!"

Rudyard Kipling knew exactly how vital drinkable water is on the battlefield, and nowhere was this more apparent than in the North African desert. In an article in the wartime propaganda magazine *Signal*, under the headline: "Travels of a Water Can", one journalist wrote:

"In Africa WATER is written in capital letters. Whoever wages war there needs water above all. Drinking water and water in the radiators of the motors ... It is a matter of course therefore, that all conversation turns round three things: water, petrol and ammunition. If there is no water the advance is held up, therefore water has to be found. There are wells, waterholes, and the sea; then there are distilling plants, both portable and stationary. As can be expected, the retreating enemy destroys all waterholes, wells, distilling apparatus and pumps; he blows them all up, batters them to pieces, dismantles them and buries the parts far below the surface of the desert. When the advance begins, the troops bring a certain amount of water with them, but not enough for the marches of hundreds of miles such as are made by Generalfeldmarschall Rommel. Water must be found, drawn and distributed among the troops so that the soldiers can drink and the radiators can be filled."

Lt Ralph Ringler wrote in his diary:

"Another wonder occurred—the sun had only just disappeared into the desert when a water wagon appeared. It was hardly possible, this wagon I had sent to El Daba ten days ago and had written off for certain; now here it was! I felt like embracing the driver. There were six old petrol barrels on board, full of brackish, petrol-flavoured, rusty water—and there was rejoicing. Three barrels were immediately

given to the field kitchen, one I kept in reserve and the other I let be distributed among the lads. Each man received four litres, the first water for a long time. We were invigorated and in high spirits. Now I could watch them—the gluttons, the spendthrifts, the thrifty, the happy.

"It all depended on the way you decided to use it. First of all a hearty slug, then I washed my face—divine! I put half a litre by for shaving, then I washed my whole body, but none was spilt. A little over a litre remained, now a murky soup. Throw it away? Not on your life! Next clothing, first a handkerchief, then my shirt and finally, in the thick dark soup, I soaked the tatters of my socks. What a day that was, it had started badly, got even worse, but now this luxury. I came out of it like a man reborn."

Even in more civilised areas water—or the lack of it—could be a problem as Otto Gunkel recalls, when, during the winter of

Above: Filling Jerricans. The robust German 20-litre (4.5 gallons) fuel can was far superior to its Allied equivalent. Fuel cans were normally painted green. Specially marked cans were used for water. (*via TRH Pictures*)

1944–45, he was in the Ruhr River dam area near Woffelsbach:

"We also had a severe lack of drinking water during January. The wells and water pipes in the villages in the battle area were all frozen. We needed to melt lots of snow to get our drinking water, but without sufficient fireplaces and jars this was a huge problem. The increasing use of phosphorous shells by the Americans poisoned the snow and that made matters worth. We also had health problems because there were no minerals in the snow we melted, but later we got salt tablets to lessen these problems."

Above: Spiritual sustenance was also necessary. (*Author's collection*)

Left: A rare treat in the desert— a convenient well. (*Author's collection*)

Below Left: Washing and shaving was usually no problem in temperate climes. (*Erich Moog*)

Below: But in some places it was perhaps better to stay dirty! (*Erich Moog*)

67

DIE GROSSE HUNGERZEIT

While one expected soldiers who were surrounded and cut off—such as those enduring the terrible hardships of the Russian winter during the siege at Stalingrad—to be short of rations, one perhaps does not think of the same happening in other more well-off areas, such as the Channel Islands. However, once the links with the mainland had been lost, military and civilian alike experienced the "Time of Great Hunger". George Brefka recalled:

"At the end of August our rations were reduced for the first time and, at the end of September, a second time. This particularly affected the bread ration, while the soup from the Company kitchen became noticeably thinner and was less nourishing … It was in October that we first felt really hungry … In November the rations were again cut and the hunger pangs worsened. The bread got worse as substitutes were mixed with the flour. We began to eat stinging nettles and grew to like them … Hunger controlled everything … owing to reduced rations the daily duties changed. Drill and exercising disappeared almost completely … In the evening the small rations were issued and gulped down ravenously. We then went straight to bed. You lay on your side, knees pulled up to the chin in order to subdue the hungry feeling."

However, such shortages, bad as they must have been, do not start to compare with those in places like Stalingrad, one survivor writing:

"More devastating than even the enemy's weapons were hunger, exhaustion, cold and illness of all kinds among the soldiers who had not been adequately fed for so many long weeks … We were lacking in food, weapons, rest, warmth, hope; in short we were lacking in all the vital conditions for fighting."

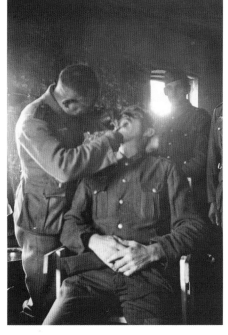
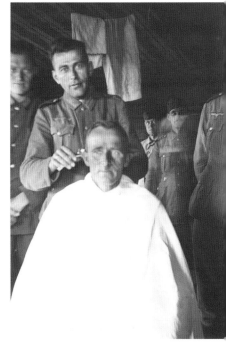

Top Left: Open wide! Dentistry in the field was often as painful as it looks. (*Erich Moog*)

Top Right: Short back and sides please. (*Erich Moog*)

Right: And there were always hungry youngsters to feed if there was anything to spare. (*Erich Moog*)

UNIFORMS

Having been issued with their initial scale of uniforms and personal equipment, a *Landser* could expect to have the major items regularly replaced whenever it was possible and the supporting services were geared up to do this—at least until the entire fabric of the army disintegrated towards the end of the war. A soldier could expect on average a new pair of socks every two months, a new shirt and new undergarments every six months, and a new uniform yearly. This extract is from a book published in Germany in 1943, entitled: *Balkenkreuz über Wüsten Sand:*

"*When we went to the base depot to get our new equipment there were those who were impatient to be photographed in their tropical helmets in the photographic studios, because our real surroundings of snow and ice at home didn't go with the new equipment. Now, however, our uniforms are grey and bleached like old camel hair. We have more sand than hair on our heads. We are bronzed; in a word we are old desert campaigners. Our uniform consisted of khaki green breeches and a coat, worn open with a khaki shirt and a cravat. I say 'consisted' as we don't wear the coats any more. The shirt sleeves are rolled up and it is bleached from washing, the sun, our sweat and the dew. Our long trousers and breeches stay in our luggage— we only wear shorts. Our high boots are made from a type of canvas, they let the air through and are very flexible. They are laced up and only the bottom part is made of hard brown leather. Even those disappear some days in the heat and soft, easy, practical lace-up shoes take their place, with green knee-length stockings. And because we are vain like all men and for some reason lay particular importance on being brown, we roll our socks down and run around whenever we can, at least half naked or even more so.*"

Top Right: Hunting in the seams for "little friends" (lice) was an essential occupation. (*Erich Moog*)

Above Right and Right: Billets came in all shapes and sizes, some with adopted helpers. (*Erich Moog*)

69

CAPTURED PROVENDER

"The night passed quietly. We obtained further things from Tommy's supply dump and slowly we became Tommies, our vehicles, petrol, rations and clothing were all English. I was somewhat international, too, with Italian shoes, French trousers, German coat and hat, English linen, stockings, gloves and blankets. A soldier's life is fine! Devoured everything, put on new linen and had some rest. Tommy, this is our revenge for the things you have done to us! Breakfasted off two tins of milk, a tin of pineapple, biscuits and Ceylon tea."

Extract from Wolfgang Everth's desert diary.

"We landed in one of the offices (just vacated in a hurry) of the Amis [Americans] who had just received parcels from home— with chocolate, sweets and a nice cake box. On one it said 'For my darling'. There was [sic] also lots of paper and letters for Christmas, but we didn't have time to read them, oh and not forgetting the cigarettes. I tried to carry too much and in my greed let half of it fall on the floor, but I also got a new pair of boots from a pile that was lying about. Then we went back to share our loot with the others. I was very happy with what I had got and packed them under my seat in the halftrack, then I started eating the chocs and sweets until I couldn't eat any more—I couldn't eat my rations either! At this moment I was enjoying the war, but we didn't know how long it would stay like this."

Extract from Guido Gneilsen's account of the opening stages of the German Ardennes offensive.

LETTERS FROM HOME

Undoubtedly regular mail from home was one of the most important aspects of maintaining good morale, so the German Field Post did all it could to ensure that mail arrived regularly whenever possible. When mail was delayed or stopped altogether, morale suffered as is evidenced by the troops occupying the Channel Islands, when during the winter 1944–45, contact with the mainland was broken.

Top and Right: Mail Call! One of the happiest days in any soldier's life was when the mail arrived—as long as there was a letter or a parcel for you! (*Erich Moog*)

70

"HOUSE OF JOY" (*FREUDENHAUS*)

The German Army took a much more relaxed view of brothels than the British Army. While there was no official policy over the opening of *Freudenhäuser* and it was left to local commanders to decide, most army officers took the view that it was far better for their soldiers to use a properly inspected brothel than to run the risk of catching venereal disease from unofficial prostitutes. For example, brothels were established in the Channel Islands for the German occupation forces, staffed by women brought over from France who were provided with civilian ration books and classed as "heavy workers!" One civilian recalled: "The queues of customers waiting in the gardens of the chosen houses afforded a certain amount of innocent amusement to the inhabitants!" A soldier's diary written in Italy contained the following comment about the local *Freudenhaus*:

"Milan's female beauties are considered more forthcoming than the girls of Sicily, who refused to associate themselves with Kuderna's men. An amicable arrangement has been reached regarding the brothels. Our divisional medical officer had declared the supervision by the Italian authorities to be excellent, and praises the business-like organisation of these houses of professional leisure which enables them to arrange a fortnightly alternative of girls."

Left: Soldiers normally travelled in "luxurious" cattle trucks. These men were part of Grenadier Battalion 398 and were moving from Goslar to Zwolle, in October 1942. (H-G. Sandmann)

Chapter 7 Medical

Every rifle platoon had someone well-trained in first aid, while within the company headquarters there was a medical (*Sanitäts*) NCO and a medical orderly, who generally worked with the battalion MO. These medics, plus additional stretcher bearers as necessary, would collect the wounded and take them to first aid 'nests' just behind the front line, where they could be given first aid and provided with transport (eg hand or vehicle stretchers) to the battalion/regimental dressing station (*Truppenverbandplatz*), staffed by the MO and two medical corpsmen. Here, the battalion MO gave the first real professional care, such as expert bandaging, splinting, applying tourniquets, injections, etc, and his post would be properly equipped with a large medical bag. Medical staff wore Red Cross armbands and were usually just armed with pistols for self-protection and that of their patients in accordance with the Geneva Convention. From the battalion/regimental aid post the wounded would be taken by ambulance sections to advanced dressing stations, then if necessary, evacuated to divisional field hospitals.

German Red Cross nurses had, on occasions, to brave artillery fire, aerial bombardment and all the other battlefield hardships, looking after the men in field hospitals, at least down to divisional level. In North Africa, for example, four nurses were awarded the Iron Cross for acts of bravery.

It should also not be forgotten that, with the large numbers of horses still employed in the German army a similar veterinarian setup was needed to deal with sick and wounded animals.

Above Right: Some battalion aid posts were in strange places, but this little dacha in Russia looks made to measure. (*Erich Moog*)

Right: First aid for a very young casualty, Poland 1941. (*Erich Moog*)

WOUNDED

"It was in mid-February 1945, when the fuse of an American anti-tank grenade almost cut off my leg near Dreiborn. I was kneeling behind a tree when the grenade impacted not far from me. I saw the fuse coming in my direction, then it hit me and my foot and boot were suddenly pointing in the wrong direction—I fainted. Later I asked a soldier to untie the tourniquet that had been put on my leg from time to time, so the blood could get into my leg again. One of my company commanders had to take over command as I kept on fainting.

"By way of several first aid posts I finally reached a hospital in the cloisters of St Ottilien at Ammersee. My military pass was the only document that I had left, and I gave it to a nurse for safe-keeping. Because of the ability of the doctors and my own determination, I was able to keep my leg—nailed together and completely stiff, but with the aid of orthopedic shoes I am able to walk."

These are the words of First Lieutenant Horst Lück, the commander of 2nd Battalion, 89th Grenadier Regiment, in an interview translated by Mr Ron van Rijt of Heerlen, in the Netherlands. This was the last and most serious of Horst Lück's wounds—he was wounded no less than eight times in all! Another of his recollections about wounds, however, concerned a self-inflicted one:

"Around 22 December 1944, a company medic brought a young soldier into our cellar, who said that he had lost the fingertip of one of his fingers of his right hand. He had probably scared himself so much that he had completely forgotten to wipe the powder-dust from his hand—self mutilation! The continuing incoming enemy artillery probably finished off his nerves, but we needed every man! I explained the situation to him and let him choose—court martial with all its consequences, or the alternative: clean the wound, disinfect it, not too thick a bandage, and become my personal attendant. Of course he agreed with the alternative. The staff said that it would be a harder punishment for him, because I was all day on the go through my unit—maybe this was still a habit from my time as a company commander."

Above Right: Even troop trains needed their medical post—in a cattle-truck, naturally! (*Erich Moog*)

Right and Far Right: First aid posts had to deal with the sick and injured as well as the battle casualties. France, 1940 and Poland 1941. (*Erich Moog*)

73

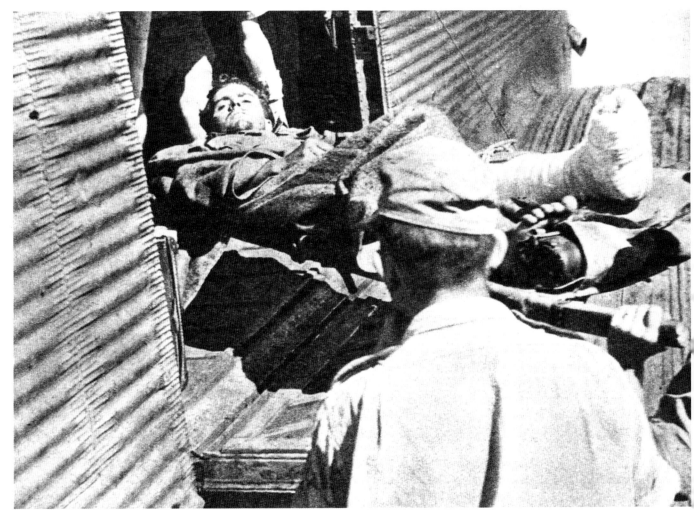

Above: Medevac. This badly wounded "Afrikan" is being loaded onto a Junkers Ju52 that will take him to hospital. (*Author's collection*)

Below: Walking wounded were also evacuated by air on occasions. (*Rolf Munninger*)

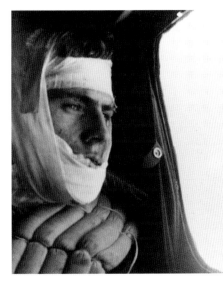

Rolf Werner Voelkers, the Panzergrenadier we met in North Africa was wounded in the desert fighting in 1942, as he recalled:

"On 31 October I was slightly wounded and landed in the field hospital [Feldlazarett] at Fuka. In hospital they found out that not only was I wounded but that I also had amoebic dysentery. We were supposed to sail on a Red Cross ship the next day, but I had a high temperature and so was classified 'too ill to travel'. Nevertheless, the following afternoon I was standing at the side of the road, with all the rest of the poor devils, a Red Cross flag in my hand, trying to get a lift as we 'waited for the Englander to arrive and take us prisoner!' After a long wait an Italian lorry pulled up and the driver started to throw out his empty petrol cans and some of his load, to make room of us. Tired, and with sore eyes, he still drove us for three days to Tobruk—I never found out who he was but to me he will always remain the 'Good Samaritan'. We were then flown out in one of the last aircraft to leave—a Focke-Wulf Fw200 Condor long-range reconnaissance bomber—to Italy and then by hospital train to Munich. I was discharged just before Christmas—which was in 1942—and because of my liver I was not allowed to serve any more in the tropics. Instead I was sent to Baumholder

where part of the Sixth Army was being rebuilt. A badly wounded major, who had been sent back from Stalingrad, was looking for chaps who had battle experience and that is how I came to be a member of an infantry light field gun unit, which was being sent out to the coal mining district of the Ukraine.

"Our first gun was already firing against the oncoming Russians before the last one was fully ready for action! And the action never stopped! However, we were soon retreating from Mius to Saporoshje on the Dnieper. My next job was in charge of ammunition and I had to go from one fire position to the next on a motorbike. As we were army troops we changed divisions more often than we changed our underclothes! In November 1943, I was caught in the Nikopol bridgehead and had to bail out of a scout car that was on fire, badly burning my hands, so I again landed in hospital—this time in the 3rd Mountain Division field hospital near Odessa. They had to treat me like a baby because I could not use my hands. Today I still give thanks to the Russian nurses who were working there for the exemplary way they treated me. I left hospital just before Christmas, 1943, and rejoined my unit in a quiet spot south of Cherson at the mouth of the Dnieper. We had time there to build a place

Above: Two medics with their distinctive Red Cross armbands use water from a jerrican—note the fact that it is painted black instead of green and has an unmistakable white cross to show that it contains water. (via TRH Pictures)

where we could get rid of our fleas and do a bit of washing. I was bath attendant as I still could not use my hands properly."

Erwin Grubba also recalled some of the horrific sights in Russia, such as when one of his comrades:

"... unfortunately trod on a mine and it blew his legs off. That was my first intimation of what war was like. And I can also still clearly see one morning, getting off the train on the side of the track, three birch tree crosses with steel helmets hanging over them with holes in them and I thought 'Ah, there's three of them that copped it.' And I can remember also seeing the first train of wounded coming back from the Kiev front ... the German Army didn't treat the soldiers to luxury trains. They were all cattle trucks with straw paliasses in them. And you saw these maimed bodies with all their bandages absolutely saturated in blood—so that wasn't a very pleasant sight."

A NURSE IN ACTION

Frau Agnes Mertes, then serving as a German Red Cross nurse, wrote:

"Our unit was ready for action at Gerolstein in the Rhineland on Christmas Eve 1944. On this very day we suffered one of the heaviest air-raids by the Allied air forces. Because of my experience as a seasoned campaigner, I was given the order to transfer the wounded soldiers from the partly destroyed hospital to an emergency sick bay that had been set up in a local inn for wounded American soldiers who had been captured. We had to care for many Americans and bedded the German wounded down in the same rooms. We also had some motor ambulances and I received another order, this time to transfer the wounded from another hospital in Büdesheim to our 'inn' in Gerolstein. The road between the two places was under heavy bombardment from Allied aircraft and when the alarm was given we had to stop, unload the wounded and hide them (and us) in the roadside ditches. One day while unloading the stretchers at our emergency hospital, a bomb exploded near the inn 'Zur Linde'. A wall caved in and fell upon the wounded soldiers and nursing staff. I was working nearby and was

Below: Back in Germany, the lucky ones were well treated in hospitals like this one at Templehof, Berlin, where Gerhard Sandmann spent from 1 March to 5 May 1942.
(H-G. Sandmann)

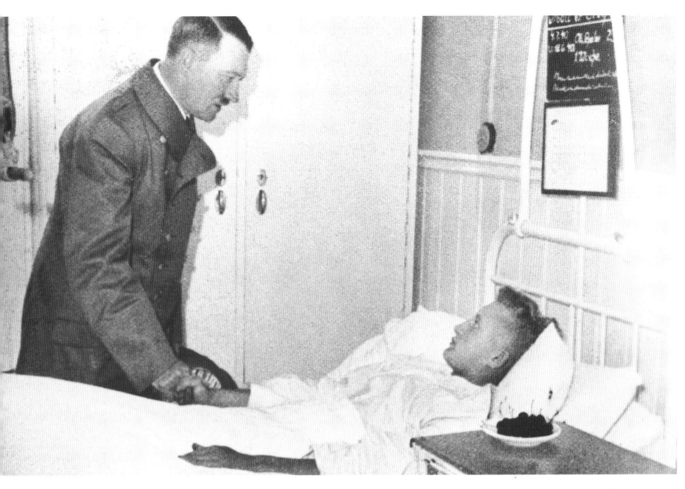

lightly wounded, but after a short treatment I was able to carry on with my duty."

THE SUPPLIES MUST GET THROUGH!

Corporal (*Obergefreiter*) Heinrich Stockoff was a member of the supply section of 1st Company, 1056th Infantry Regiment, who were responsible for getting hot food up to the front lines. In November 1944, they were in the Eifel prior to the Ardennes offensive, as he recalls:

"On 18 November the kitchen units moved from Rurberg to Abenden. Now began our worst time in the Eifel. It rained every day and we were always wet through. At least from Abenden we could drive through the protection of the forest and then to the east to reach the road to Heimbach from

Above: The Führer even visited some casualties in the early days. This one was wounded in the Battle for France in May/June 1940. (Author's collection)

Left: Out for the first time. Gerhard Sandmann in Berlin, May 1942, while an in-patient at Templehof Hospital. (H-G. Sandmann)

Schmidt. To the southeast of Schmidt was a German artillery position, the target of American counter-battery fire. So on the 18th we kept getting shelled in Schmidt. Even the road from Schmidt to Gerstenhof gave us little protection. Schmidt was almost totally destroyed and we could hardly get through the place. Then further enemy artillery fire on the 19th blocked the way completely, so we had to use a southerly detour to reach Gerstenhof. On the 24th we took more artillery fire between Schmidt and Gerstenhof. *Unteroffizier* [Sergeant] Wagener hid in a ditch, *Obergefreiter* Ludwig Kirchenlohr and I successfully galloped our horses and the supply vehicles away from the bombardment. Afterwards Wagener said, 'How could you leave me alone in a ditch?'

"On the 25th the last service took place in St Martin's Church, Abenden, because the civilian population was evacuated afterwards. I was able to take Mass that morning and Wagener said to me, 'Say a prayer for me, too.' The company had to supply Buhlert that afternoon, but we got lost in the Hürtgen Forest. Because we then had to waste more time turning around, Wagener told me and Kirchenlohr to go ahead while he got the food ready. We had reached the western exit of the forest on the way to Schmidt when we were hit by more shellfire—the first shell exploding in our midst. One of our horses—'Liesel'—was wounded in both legs; another—'Fuchs'—

was killed. Kirchenlohr was hit in the left foot by shrapnel, I was hit twice in my right arm, one splinter going through the lower part of the arm, while another piece was left sticking out of my upper arm. I took cover in the crater of the shell that had hit us and my badly bleeding wounds were bound up by one of the Luftwaffe troops who had been detailed to escort us. I was taken to safety in an artillery bunker (Bunker 720 at Simonsley) where there was an officer and a medical orderly who dressed my arm. Kirchenlohr had, in the meantime, ridden the wounded 'Liesel' to Battalion HQ and reported our misfortunes. We later learnt from Sgt. Wagener that the company got its full rations, apart from cigarettes. The officer in the bunker said to me: 'This evening our supply vehicle is due and you can get back to Heimbach with them.'

"After a while I told the two vehicle drivers of the supply vehicle that my wounds hurt more when I sat, so I walked behind the vehicle [clearly the vehicle was a horse and cart which must have been extremely uncomfortable]. Where the road forked I went left and got back through the wood to my unit at Abenden. Sgt Wagener was pretty impressed when I told him what had happened. I finally reached the main aid station at Froitzheim, where the shrapnel was taken out of my upper arm. Then on 27 November (my mother's birthday) I reached the hospital in Rengsdorf, Westerwald, where I would convalesce."

Chapter 8 R & R

HOME ON LEAVE

As the photographs show, some soldiers, while they were serving in the occupation role, were allowed short leave periods to such world-famous tourist attractions as Paris. However, they were also all allowed, whenever possible, home leave—even from such faraway places as the Eastern Front. Every officer and soldier was entitled to 14 days home leave every year, on top of which, in special circumstances, compassionate leave or convalescence, after wounding or serious illness, were possible for limited periods. Thus a fair percentage—up to 10 percent according to some estimates—of German soldiers were on leave at any one time—how different from the British Army where home leave was normally just a distant dream! For most of the war this enlightened leave policy was maintained and it was the exception to find a soldier who had not been home once in every year of his service—at least until 1945, when all such well-regulated procedures began to unravel. Every soldier on leave was required to report back immediately should he have to be suddenly recalled—failure to do so and to remain absent without leave could mean a death sentence when caught. However, most soldiers went back willingly enough, having found it difficult to relate to family life after months with their "army family".

Above: A favourite place for R&R ("Rest & Relaxation" or "Rack & Ruin"!) leave was obviously Paris. Here three soldiers pause in their sightseeing under the shadow of the Arc de Triomphe du Carousel in the grounds of the Louvre. (*H-G. Sandmann*)

Left: In some of the open-air "flea" markets, stall holders who could speak German advertised the fact, as did this Rumanian stallholder. (*H-G. Sandmann*)

OÙ EST LA TOILETTE?

"Talmay Castle was a large, well-cared for building. There didn't seem to be anyone in charge, but the servants had stayed in place and one of them took us to our rooms. The Flivo-kommando and I were billeted on the third or fourth floor of a huge tower. It was a round room of considerable size; right in the middle of it, the focal point was a double bed with a canopy. I checked to see that my men were all sorted out and then went to claim the inviting bedstead, only to find that Tunnes had taken it over. Elsewhere on sofas and couches, Moser, Kaiser, Heinrich and Fritz Heschel had made themselves comfortable.

"It was very difficult later on to summon up the energy to go downstairs to eat. In fact I snaffled a couple of good bottles from the table and went upstairs again. It was a wonderful red wine. I didn't go out. I just stayed in that fantastic canopied bed to the accompaniment of Tunnes' snores. It was not a quiet night! We all had drunk well and slept well for it. In the last five weeks none of us had had more than four hours sleep a day—but despite this, even the deepest sleep cannot stop the workings of a wine-filled bladder. And that's what mine did; and as hard as I tried to stay asleep, so my bladder ached more—I had to go!

"But where was the lavatory? I had no idea. I took a chance on finding it and left the room. I wandered about darkened corridors, pushed carefully on mighty door handles, but all I could find were other rooms, chambers, cabinets—everything but a loo!

"Holy Sacks of Cement! I was about to go in my trousers and at the same time I had also lost myself completely and didn't know how to get back to my room. Luckily I held on and did find my room again. What to do? I pulled the window up and urinated out of it, letting out a great sigh of satisfaction as my bladder was relieved.

"Then I had a shock. There was a great drumming sound. I shook the last alcoholic haze from my brain and realised what was going on. I was relieving myself onto a lead roof and in the still of the night the noise must have reached the depths of the deepest forest. Then I heard a screeching voice: 'Monsieur, la toilette se trouve as fin du couloir a droit!' [Sir, the lavatory is at the end of the corridor on the right!]

"At last I got back to sleep again, but not for as long as I would have liked—at 1000 hours the division reassembled."

Left: One of the highspots of R&R in "Gay Paree" was a visit to "Les Folies". (*H-G. Sandmann*)

Below: Another, larger group of sightseers, pause under the Obelisk. Gerhard Sandmann visited Paris on 10 August 1941, some months before his division was sent to the Russian Front. (*H-G. Sandmann*)

Above: And after leave comes the inevitable goodbye at the station— especially poignant as these soldiers of 216th Infantry Division will soon be on the way to Russia, in December 1941. (*H-G. Sandmann*)

OTHER STORIES

Panzergrenadier Rolf Volkers recalled:

"In the Siebenbürgen, a German settlement for over 800 years, I met in Bistrtz, a lovely blonde, blue-eyed girl—sweet 17 and her name was Erika. It was one of the happiest days of my life that, after many hard years, she became my wife on 3 August 1957. Erika and her family were 'on the trek' for two months, because in September 1944, together with all the other German families, they were evacuated with their all belongings on just one horse and cart. At that time I was with my regiment in Chemnitz, Saxony. My flat in Stuttgart had been bombed out. This was in July. In October I got a bit of leave and was caught in two air-raids."

Postwar, on his release from POW camp, Rolf would return to live in his bombed-out flat in Stuttgart and eventually he and his beloved Erika would be married.

Werner Wagenknecht managed just one period of home leave during his sojourn in the Channel Islands and it coincided with some of the worst early bombing on Berlin as he recalls:

"You asked me if I went on leave while staying in Guernsey—yes, I did, but just one time only! It was when the great bombing attacks on Berlin illuminated my return to Guernsey, after I had seen the daffodils blooming in my mother's garden, which I had sent her as bulbs the year before, by air mail from the Channel Islands."

Above Right and Right: For the married soldiers, home leave was eagerly awaited. Here Erich Moog spends a few days with his family in May 1942, after a year on the Russian front. (Erich Moog)

Far Right: *"Auf Wiedersehen Liebchen."* (H-G. Sandmann)

Chapter 9 Army of Occupation

Above: Everyone loves to hear a band—this is one of 216th Infantry Division's regimental bands and it is playing in one of the recently occupied towns in Normandy—possibly Granville or Cherbourg—prior to the division's occupation of the Channel Islands. (H-G. Sandmann)

ON THE CHANNEL ISLANDS

Erwin Grubba recalled his arrival in Guernsey on a tape (No 10006/8) for the Imperial War Museum's Sound Archive:

"My first impression of the Channel Islands was the peaceful atmosphere in the morning, arriving at St Peter Port and seeing the first British bobby in a dark blue uniform with his tall hat. And notices advertising Fyffe's bananas and Mazwatee tea. I knew I was on a good ticket here.

"It was like ordinary garrison duty of any military body, the usual guard duties, guarding depots, and of course, Hitler had built huge fortifications all along the coastline, with concrete bunkers that had to be manned day and night. Units were dispersed all over the Channel Islands, not only in the coastal areas, but with training units, munitions depots, etc. Belonging to an infantry regiment, we had to man a particular sector of Guernsey called Vazon Bay, which is probably now a beautiful summer resort, with lovely beaches … After our arrival we were marched to our various billets and very soon the ordinary routine began—stand-to in the morning, parades and night duties, most of the guard duties

being shift work. You went on duty an manned these concrete bunkers at nigh time. You went off again at six o'clock in th morning and took your guard duties as the came.

"Plus drill exercises—a lot of militar exercises went on in the island, to the grea annoyance sometimes of the farmers n doubt. Because as it got later and later i the war, and the fear of invasion becam more acute, they had these anti-parachut bombs on these wooden pegs rammed int the ground in the fields, among the shee and cattle. And, of course as you know, th Jersey and Guernsey cattle are very famous so it didn't suit the farmers much becaus one of the cows might hit a wire or rub i neck against one of the posts and the whol shoot blow up and it could be killed. I thin it did happen occasionally.

"As far as I could tell, being able t converse with the people quite wel although my English wasn't that good . but I soon made contact, going into shop buying grapes and tomatoes and what-no And the people were—I think the best wa to put it is, absolutely 'correct'. They wer downright loyal to the Crown. Of cours they didn't owe anything to Westminst and Parliament, but they were dire subjects to the Crown—they were loyal

Left: Led by their band, men of Infantry Regiment 398 march through Zwolle in early 1943. (*H-G. Sandmann*)

Left and Below Left: Most of the entertainment was arranged by the troops themselves while they were relaxing in their billets, such as singsongs and parties. (*H-G. Sandmann*)

Below: Initially, the occupation troops got on quite well with the local population, as seen here in Normandy, July 1940. (*H-G. Sandmann*)

the King and Queen in those days and they made no bones about that. They had pictures of the Royal Family in their parlours, over their settees. And they always told you: 'We are subjects of the King. We're not British, we're Guernsey people, but we are loyal to the King and of course we naturally hope and pray for an Allied victory.'

"They made no bones about that and somehow that created mutual respect. One felt they were neither collaborators nor cringers or taking advantage of the situation. I think they behaved extremely well and they were sensible too ... The farmer I was friendly with, near my billet, always used to say: 'I love your singing when you march off in the morning on your exercises. It sounds great. But by gum, I wish you would go all the same. Because it will be nice to be free again.'

"But of course let's not forget it. They were lucky. The administration, the military government of the island, was again not of the Nazi type. They were people like von Schmettow [Generalleutnant Graf von Schmettow—liberal-minded commander of the Islands for most of war until he was summarily 'retired' and rabid Nazi Vizeadmiral Friedrich Hüffmeier took over] ... They were not the rough and rowdy type, definitely they [sic: the islanders] were lucky in that way. They got on quite well."

Right: A group of infantrymen take a rest under the shadow of a dry stone wall, during a route march. (via TRH Pictures)

Below: Off-duty soldiers relax beside one of Guernsey's many bays. (H-G. Sandmann)

MIXED RESISTANCE

Naturally, the occupation of the rest of Europe was not always carried out with such equanimity as in the Channel Islands, which some historians have described as being "the model occupation".

Undoubtedly there was at one end of the scale, active hostility and opposition to German rule, highlighted by the growth of such organisations as the French Maquis; while at the other there was equally active collaborationism, together with the wholehearted support and acceptance of fascism by some members of the population. The four-year German occupation is still referred to by some people in France as the "four years to strike from our history."

Further east, in countries like Poland, the civil population was treated with such casual brutality as to foster resistance among most sections of the population. Active resistance, such as sabotage, helping others to escape and collecting/passing on useful intelligence, was, when discovered, always dealt with harshly by the occupying forces, while there were many forms of passive resistance, which probably was just as effective in the long run.

Above: In most areas, the Wehrmacht produced its own newspapers so that soldiers could keep abreast of the approved local and worldwide news. These two soldiers are in Guernsey. Unteroffizier Werner Wagenknecht is wearing his marksmanship lanyard. (W. Wagenknecht)

Left: In some locations soldiers were billeted in requisitioned houses, while in others they had barrack room accommodation as here in Tournai, France. (H-G. Sandmann)

However, it has to be said that most of the active work against those who resisted was carried out by the "experts" in that field, rather than the average garrison soldier, who would normally try to remain at arm's length from the civilian population. This was easy to do when billeted in a barracks, but more difficult when they lived for months, or even years, cheek by jowl, right among the civilian population. Oberst Baron von Aufsess in his *Occupation Diary* on 13 September 1944, wrote:

"I am greatly depressed by Oberstleutnant Helldorf's failure to follow the reasoning of my memorandum, he just tries to make light of the matter and patch up the situation … Against the General's wishes, he has taken that girl to Guernsey, where she is now living with him … His intention must be to hold out as long as possible to try to achieve at the end a free withdrawal of German troops from the island. Only in these circumstances would he be able to take the girl back with him to Germany. He intends, in the total derangement of his senile infatuation, to marry this little servant-girl. So do the private concerns of the individual affect the welfare of the many."

Right: Garrison duties had to be performed, like these sentries on duty outside their battalion HQ in Zwolle, Holland. (*H-G. Sandmann*)

Below: Office accommodation was sometimes good and sometimes bad, but I doubt if many battalions had such palatial offices as this one in Zwolle. (*H-G. Sandmann*)

Chapter 10 The End in Africa

EL ALAMEIN

We left Rommel and his "Afrikans" facing the Eighth Army at El Alamein/Alam Halfa. in late June 1942. apparently about to break through to Cairo and the Suez Canal.

It was not to be. The Eighth Army held their positions and Rommel was forced back onto the defensive. Soon it was the Allies' turn to take the offensive. Suitably reinforced. Montgomery attacked on the night of 23–24 October and after a week of heavy fighting. the Axis forces broke and began to withdraw. The battle of El Alamein was heralded as one of the turning points of the war. As always. Hitler had intervened in early November. issuing one of his "No Retreat" orders. which prevented Rommel from extricating his troops properly, although it was rescinded after two days. One of the German soldiers. whose company was guarding the exits from one of the many defensive minefields along the front. as the massive opening barrage crashed down onto their positions recalled:

"The day seemed never-ending. I crawled from strong point to strong point and everywhere there were anxious, tired faces, asking me questions for which I had no answer. I tried to get rations up to the posts, but after hours of waiting, the food carrier eventually arrived carrying just packets of hermetically sealed: 'Afrika Brot,' tubes of cheese and cold coffee—it was disgraceful!"

"The battle which began at El Alamein on 23 October 1942 turned the tide of war in Africa against us and, in fact, probably represented the turning point of the whole vast struggle."

So wrote Rommel in his diary. putting the importance of the El Alamein into perspective. Four days later he wrote to his wife:

"A very hard struggle. No one can conceive the burden that lies on me. Everything is at stake again and we're fighting under the greatest possible handicaps. However, I hope we will pull through. You know I'll put all I've got into it."

At the same time he commented bitterly in his diary about Hitler's "No Retreat" order: "Arms. petrol and aircraft could have helped us. but not orders." From then on he was forced. on occasions. to circumvent such missives from Hitler in order to save his army from destruction—something which he would never have contemplated doing before.

Above: The El Alamein barrage begins. Hour after hour the British guns pounded the German positions. (*Author's collection*)

Below: Burning vehicles litter the desert as the DAK begins its stubborn withdrawal. (*Rolf Munninger*)

THE GREAT WITHDRAWAL

There followed a long, hard-fought pursuit across Cyrenaica and all the way to the Mareth Line, which was reached on 13 February 1943. Rommel calls it the "Great Retreat", however, that is perhaps being hard on his soldiers, who actually carried out an orderly withdrawal, which at no time became a rout. With considerable skill, fighting doggedly and making all possible use of demolitions and booby traps, Panzerarmee Afrika withdrew through North Africa. They were controlled by the "iron hand" of Rommel all the way, and, despite the fact that he was sick both in heart and body, he did so with consummate skill.

"We blew up culverts and bridges at every wadi and strewed mines along the route. The enemy had to push along cautiously … Our old weary business of leapfrogging backwards, laying mines and blowing demolitions went on again." These two short comments are from Hauptmann Heinz Werner Schmidt, who was at one time part of Rommel's personal staff, but was now back with his infantry regiment, commanding a special all-arms group during the withdrawal. He also says: "Without question his [Rommel's] economical retreat with the remnants of the Afrika Korps from El Alamein to the Mareth Line was one of his greatest, though probably least appreciated, achievements as a tactical leader." Before the withdrawal could begin, however, they had to make a "clean break."

"The desert and the glowing wrecks now had an exciting effect, once more there was an objective—a new spirit woke inside us." That is how Lt Ralph Ringler, whom we met full of excitement just after he had volunteered to serve in North Africa a few months previously [see Chapter 4] and, now a desert-hardened warrior, was about to begin what is possibly the hardest of all

military operations to carry out successfully, namely an ordered withdrawal. He continued:

"In a few moments, my section and group commanders have arrived for my briefing—that is those who are not wounded, and they have sent their deputies. We must make our withdrawal quickly and silently, because the enemy mustn't know that we have withdrawn, at least until we are well clear. One group after another has to crawl over the edge of the dune, then through the minefield by the safe path, collecting together at the far side. I sent my driver with the first group so that he could drive to our now vacated observation post, to collect the dead as we wanted to take them with us. The wounded who couldn't walk would be carried out on the assault gun. Feldwebel Fiedler and I would stay until after the last group had gone, then we would spike the damaged anti-tank gun as it could no longer be towed out.

"Getting the men fully awake and ready to move was the worst job. Those not on duty were sleeping like the dead. We had to hit them with our fists, but after a lot of quiet, but determined, urging we managed to get them to move. One major problem was shifting the undamaged anti-tank gun that had to be manhandled up a steep dune. Breathing heavily, then struggling for breath, we all tried our best to move the heavy gun up and over the dune. It took us over 20 minutes, but at last we managed it. The men were exhausted, they collapsed behind the dune as if they were dead.

"I then had to go back to the position to check that all had left—the wounded were still there plus one last group of about six men. Then, heralded only by a short whistling that gave us no time to take cover, in came a shell, causing a shattering explosion right beside us. Gunner Lukas cried out and clutched at a foot; Kater fell and stayed down, so I crawled over to him.

His face was ashen. A pool of blood started to collect under his Feldmütze [side cap]. As carefully as possible I lifted off the cap and saw immediately that a shell splinter had torn away part of his scalp on the back of his head. But he was still alive and looking at me, he moaned softly. 'Does it hurt Kater?' I asked. He shook his head slightly but could not speak.

"Had the English seen our movement or was this just part of their routine shelling? One could not tell, but all the more reason for getting away as quickly as possible. We put an explosive charge down the barrel of the second anti-tank gun, had a final good look all round and then I sent off the last, sad procession. Kater was tied to the outside of the assault gun. Lukas, thank goodness, only had a flesh wound. They had roped the serviceable anti-tank gun on behind the assault gun and at last, when all was ready, they set off. Hopefully they would be able to get through the minefield safely. Then I told Fiedler to light the fuse and, that done, there was no reason for us to remain. No doubt Tommy would twig sooner or later—hopefully later—that something was up.

"It was now some three hours since the first of us had left and I reckoned that it was about midnight, but both our watches had stopped. We were lying down behind the dunes, next to us were the three corpses—Monier, Hanke and Bauer. The moon had risen by now, turning the entire desert into a silver, shimmering landscape. We tried to sleep, but couldn't. We heard the crack of the explosive charge in the anti-tank gun. If Tommy heard it then there wasn't anything we could do about it. If only the car would arrive! It didn't appear that the enemy had heard the explosion, or if they had they weren't taking any notice. Then I heard a noise and nudged Fiedler. Was it the English coming? Then I saw my car appearing out of the minefield. The driver was shaking uncontrollably, the journey through the minefield had really shaken him up. 'I can't

Left: Detailed planning of each and every stage of the slow fighting withdrawal was absolutely essential. (*Author's collection*)

Right: DAK MG34 position, with the 7.92mm weapon in heavy machine gun mode mounted on a tripod. (*Author's collection*)

drive back,' he said, so I had to. We carried the three dead bodies in the back, with a tarpaulin over them. They were motionless and stiff, with just their feet were visible over the edge of the car.

"The moon was behind us and all I could see was the shadow of the three pairs of feet in the sand, right next to me. Fiedler sat beside me, with the car driver standing on the running board beside him. I drove very slowly, trying to keep to the tracks of the assault gun. Once I thought I had lost the track completely, then I thought the corpses had rolled off. Again and again I looked at the shadows of the feet to make sure they were still there. We kept on hitting patches of soft sand that slowed us down and I could smell the clutch burning out. The cold moon landscape, the burning oil smell from the clutch, the monotonous grinding of the wheels, the shadows of the feet—they just went on and on. I never realised how long eight kilometres could be. I felt that the journey would never end and it was all affecting my already strained nerves, especially the shadows of those dead men's feet!

"Were they alive? The shadows certainly looked alive, but the men were dead. I started—I must have fallen asleep—how long—hours or just seconds? Fiedler was asleep beside me but the driver was awake. 'The company—we're through!' I stopped, exhausted, my hands dropping from the steering wheel. My head was heavy and thick. 'Get a grip!' I told myself, 'You are the leader of these men!' I got out of the seat with difficulty and walked around. I tried to speak, but nothing came, just a soundless caving in my throat. The assault gun wasn't there it had driven on; There were about 30 men of my company here and we lay down on the cold, hard sand.

"When dawn came I awoke. My first thought was of the six stiff feet in the moonlight. Mein Gott! I hadn't lost my dead—or was everything that lay around me dead? Then I saw the car, Fiedler sleeping and the three stiff figures in the back.

"Then there came the noise of engines and three Volkswagens with three smart, washed and rested drivers arrived. I personally drove my car with the three corpses back to our old Company HQ and then on to battalion. I didn't let them out of my sight as I reported. In spite of everything they would stay in the desert for ever, becoming the dust and sand of the desert."

REARGUARD

Hauptmann Heinz Werner Schmidt was a member of a special force. Known as Special Force 288, it was deliberately left out of the battle because it was to be Rommel's rearguard. He recalled later:

"When the last of the Panzers rolled westward, our task began. We were to be Rommel's rearguard. We pulled out last of all, and had retreated only a few miles along the coast road when we were engaged by armoured cars immediately south of the road. Our guns went into action and we fought them off.

"The Special Group moved back in leapfrog movements. One battalion was always halted in defensive positions to cover the retreat and then it would 'up guns' and off. We reached Mersa Matruh on 6 November. I was ordered to take up temporary positions on Matruh's southern defence line and on both sides of the Siwa track. I sited anti-tank guns—each of my companies had five or six of these—at the most important points. Our positions lay between the bunkers where the barbed-wire entanglements and minefields had been left intact as they had been when Auchinleck's men had sought to hold this line. Late that afternoon I sighted British tanks on a rise south of Matruh. As darkness fell they opened fire on my positions along the oasis track. The pursuit was relentless. Under cover of darkness the surviving columns of our Panzer groups left the stronghold and resumed their westward march."

Schmidt then received a written situation report and orders brought by a DR, which gave him details of the latest developments. From them he learnt that Montgomery's spearheads were already west of Matruh. The orders told him to be ready to abandon his present rearguard positions from midnight and gave him a compass bearing to the only remaining safe lane through the minefield. Schmidt regretted the fact that he had not been given the chance to locate it in daylight and to mark on his map the all important entrance to the minefield. However, at least they would have the opportunity of evading capture, which would have been inevitable had they remained outside Matruh for much longer.

"My driver and the dispatch-rider blacked out my truck with blankets. By the glow of a little bulb wired off a battery, we swallowed a meal from cans and wrote letters home. Busy writing, I failed to notice that midnight had come and long since gone. Then the 'Phutt! Phutt!' of a motorcycle. The machine stopped and a voice called out: 'Is that Special Group 288?' A hoarse whisper: 'Shut up! Tommy can probably hear you!' The dispatch-rider was led to me. A hand thrust through the blackout blankets. A voice repeated the written order I read: 'Matruh evacuated. Rearguard to follow immediately!'"

By then Schmidt had the drill off pat. Each of the sub-units in the battalion had an

Above: The MG42, seen mounted on a bipod in its light role, had a higher rate of fire than the MG34—up to 1,500 rpm—and was an ideal weapon for ambushing or delaying the enemy. (*Author's collection*)

Above Left: This Oberleutnant's forage cap looks as if it has a Gebirgsjäger insignia—an Edelweiss—on its side. If this is the case, then it is unlikely the photograph was taken in Africa as the closest the Gebirgsjäger got to was Crete, which was not retaken by the Allies until 1944. (*via TRH Pictures*)

Left: Another Orders Group, another plan for another ambush, as the DAK withdrew across the deserts of North Africa. (*Colonel T. Bock*)

Right: Dusty and dishevelled, the "Desert Fox" was still an inspiration to his "Afrikans". (*Rolf Munninger*)

orderly who was detailed to wait with his vehicle by the command truck. It took only a few moments to pass on the orders and very quickly they were speeding back to the gun positions. Then "Limber up—load ammunition" and everyone converged on Schmidt's position, to form up close by. However, Schmidt was not very pleased, because there had been too much noise and shouting as the drivers called to one another. The inevitable followed—a barrage of tank shells! Some of the trucks were hit and burst into flames. What to do? Surveying the scene, Schmidt came to the conclusion that there weren't many enemy tanks, however, it would be pointless, nay, impossible, to dismount and dig in. They must pull out as ordered. However, just in case they did have to stop and dig in, he tucked an entrenching tool under the strap across his shoulder—later this could almost cause disaster, but at the time it seemed a sensible thing to do.

"'In extended intervals—march!' I shouted the order and standing in my truck, kept my eyes on the compass needle so as to navigate through the darkness to the minefield gap. We drove through a minor storm of enemy shells. The drivers had only one aim—to get out of range of the pursuing tanks and their convoy discipline faltered. Contrary to orders the trucks closed in upon each other and sometimes even raced side by side, despite the extended-order drill. Gradually the shelling petered out. I was about to draw a sigh of relief when there was a roar and a jolt. My truck lurched to a stop, radiator and engine smashed!"

Hauptmann Schmidt immediately thought that there must be more enemy tanks up ahead. The only thing to do was to keep going and drive through the enemy blocking position. Schmidt and his driver, who had been slightly wounded, leapt off their truck and onto the vehicle that was immediately behind.

"'Forward, don't deviate!' I yelled at the driver. But there was no forward dash for that truck. Again that flash, crash and jolt. The driver and two other men in the truck were wounded. Though I was sitting in the cab too, I escaped unscathed."

Again he leapt out and at once saw two more brilliant flashes and heard two more explosions off to the right. He shouted to his men to dismount and dig in, then saw that they were doing this already. Every vehicle had halted and the men were already flat on the ground. However, apart from their own engine noise there was no other sound. From time to time a few shells screamed overhead from the pursuing tanks, which had all but given up the chase—but where was the enemy who had been firing at them from in

Above: More Axis prisoners of war, including both Germans and Italians, on board captured transport at Enfidaville. (*Author's collection*)

Left: Left in the desert are the graves of those who were killed en route from El Alamein to Tunis. (*Major D. Mitchell*)

Right: There were medals for bravery for some—to be presented at ad hoc ceremonies in the desert. (*Colonel T. Bock*)

front? Then he realised—they had hit the minefield. But how? His compass reading had been dead accurate, despite their speed he could swear that he had read it correctly. Then he realised, the steel spade had caused the needle to deviate. He threw the damned entrenching tool away and took another bearing, and, as he had expected, the needle now pointed much farther to the left.

"I had been foolish. Here we now were in the middle of a minefield, with enemy tanks hard behind us. It was up to me to retrieve the situation. I wrapped my mind in calmness, made my plan, and, with the men lying prone, stepped out to look for the edge of the minefield."

Schmidt was helped by one of his men, who only a few days before had been found guilty of stealing from a comrade and been called a *Schweinhund* by Schmidt on a battalion parade. He, regardless of the obvious danger, now ran about, looking at the vehicle tracks and locating mines. There did not appear to be any anti-personnel mines, just the large anti-tank/vehicle type and soon they located the edge of the minefield and found the gap—they had missed it by some 50 yards. Only the leading vehicles of the column were inside the minefield. While part of the battalion took up a defensive position, others manhandled the vehicles still at risk to the gap. Only one mine exploded and no one was killed, nor was there any enemy interference. However, it took two hours to get the column properly aligned and moving safely on through the gap. They had lost four vehicles, but none of the men had been killed. When they reached the far end of the gap they were met by a squad of anxious engineers, waiting to mine the gap as soon as Schmidt's party had passed safely through.

"The first rays of the sun were on our backs and casting exaggerated shadows in front of us as a swarm of bombers roared low overhead. I extended my column swiftly but the airmen ignored us. Had they mistaken us, I wondered, for the British vanguard? Then, on the far horizon we saw them dive and drop their bombs. We now knew where the main body of the Afrikakorps was."

By mid-February 1943, Montgomery's Eighth Army had pushed the Axis forces right back to the Mareth Line in southern Tunisia. British and Commonwealth forces began a frontal assault a month later, but the Axis forces under the Italian Marshal Giovanni Messe, managed to hold them until the New Zealand Corps, under General Freyberg, carried out a "left hook" through the Tebaga Gap on 27 March. Now the battleground was Tunisia.

OPERATION TORCH AND AFTER

Meanwhile in November 1942, Anglo-American landings (Operation Torch) had taken place in Vichy French North Africa, thus placing the Allied First Army behind the German and Italian forces. Kesselring did manage to get some reinforcements to Tunisia, and the Germans and their Italian partners did have some early successes—despite having to fight on two fronts. One of these major battles was at Kasserine Pass, where, for the very first time, the Germans faced the Americans. US II Corps, contained some 30,000 eager young soldiers, thirsting for action but without any battle experience and led by senior officers who had last fought on the battlefields of France in 1918.

Facing them were Rommel's battle-hardened veterans, who had fought over the length of North Africa against Montgomery's Eighth Army, together with Generaloberst Jürgen von Arnim's Panzerarmeeoberkommando 5, whose main troops were the 10th Panzer Division, which had been transferred from France to Tunisia in late November 1942. There was little love lost between the aristocratic von Arnim and Rommel, whom it is said he described as being, "that upstart Swabian". Rommel was far from well, having only recently returned from a short period of sick-leave in Germany. Nevertheless, he quickly regained some of his old bounce and verve, as did his soldiers at his return. "You should have seen their eyes light up when he suddenly appeared," wrote Rommel's aide to Frau Rommel, "It was just like the old days, amongst the foremost infantry and tanks, in the midst of their attack, he hit the dirt just like the riflemen when the enemy's artillery opened up!"

The Germans launched their first concerted attack on 19 February. While other units tried to force a passage further to the north, Rommel concentrated his forces with the aim of taking the vital Kasserine Pass on the following day. The DAK literally smashed its way through a much larger American force, inflicting heavy casualties. One onlooker described the scene as being like "a picture of hell right before our eyes".

The German operations had started some days before with a two-pronged assault, the first being Operation *Frühlingswind* (Spring Breeze) by von Arnim's 10th and 11th Panzer Divisions, launched on 14 February through the Faid Pass onto Sidi bou Zid. Then on the 16th came the DAK through Gafsa in Operation *Morgenluft* (Morning Air). Unfortunately, there was little co-ordination between the two assaults, von Arnim merely wanting to make limited improvements to his forward positions, while Rommel's aim on the other

hand was to cause as much damage as possible to the "green" Americans, which he hoped would have considerable repercussions for the future. If their luck held, they might even be able to blitz their way through the Allied rear areas and reach the main bases at Bone and Constantine—and what chaos that would cause!

One of the units involved in these battles was the 104th Infantry Regiment, whose Machine Gun Battalion's diary recorded its progress thus:

"Our battalion marched off on 13 February with 21st Panzer Division who had been relieved of the Faid Pass ... we pushed through Gunifidia, southwards, swinging around Sidi Mecheri, then northwest to Bir el Afey on the main road from Gafsa to Sidi bou Zid. Moving on from there we reached a dried up wadi west of Zafria—about 14km west of Sidi bou Zid by the early morning of the 14th."

They then found themselves between two formidable American positions at Sid bou Zid and Gafsa. Initially all was quiet and they were able to take up positions facing northward without any interference. However, not for long!

"At about 0100 hours our eyes literally 'jumped out of their sockets' and we caught our breath as a huge wedge of enemy tanks came towards us! Undaunted, No 1 Company's new 7.5cm anti-tank gun started the battle, but it had not been particularly well sited and the clouds of dust, which were thrown up every time it fired, soon gave away its position and it was knocked out by two direct hits."

The American tanks now knew the location of the DAK troops, however, instead of continuing their advance they halted in the open and were subjected to a ferocious artillery barrage, while tanks of the 1st and 7th Panzer Regiments outflanked them on both sides, under cover of the tall cacti and camel thorn. Then all hell broke loose!

"Our Panzerschützen [anti-tank guns] fired shot after shot; yelling and explosions filled the air; tanks were burning, enveloped by dense clouds of black smoke, while others exploded, and some turned in circles, with one track destroyed, aimlessly firing all the while. Then the Luftwaffe joined in the attack and the inferno mounted—a picture of hell right before our eyes.

"In the evening we counted 34 Shermans lying knocked out on the battlefield, still glowing redly. We sent foot patrols to search the area and took nearly 80 prisoners, who all belonged to the American 1st Armoured Division. This had been their first action and they were

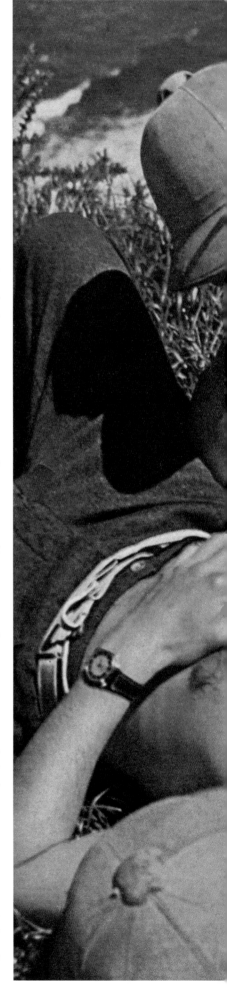

exhausted, most going to sleep as soon as they reached our lines."

The heavy tank battle would continue on the 15th as the enemy were forced back with more heavy casualties. In total some 150 American tanks and other armoured vehicles were knocked out in the two days, while approximately 2,000 GIs were taken prisoner. Unfortunately for the Germans this success was not followed up immediately and the Axis forces did not move on again until the 17th. The unofficial war diary continues:

"We marched away from Sidi bou Zid in darkness. The track led northwestwards about five kilometres away from the parallel main road to Sbeitla ... at the front of the column was No 3 Company, commanded by the young and intense Lt Boy, who was always pushing forward. We lost contact with them during the night, so Hauptmann Kuhn sent two members of the Signal Platoon forward in a captured jeep to re-establish contact."

At the head of the battalion column was a *Schützenpanzerwagen* (an armoured personnel carrier)—the only one the battalion possessed. It was armed with two machine guns, one at the front with an armoured shield and one at the back on an AA mounting. The battalion adjutant, Lt Starke, was manning the front machine gun, when suddenly off to his right front he saw groups of figures among the camel thorn and cactus, clearly moving across towards the battalion's route. He also saw the captured jeep with the two Signal Platoon personnel in it on its return journey. Then he heard shots and could see that the jeep was surrounded by a group of men whose olive drab uniforms and spherical helmets clearly showed them to be Americans.

"Alarm! Shooting was impossible at that moment for fear of hitting the crew of the jeep. Hauptmann Kuhn was told of the strength of the enemy and sent Nos 1 and 3 Companies, who had been at the head of the column, to the left of the track so as to stop any further westward movement by the enemy. Oberleutnant Batt and his No 5 Company was immediately sent to the right of the track to take the enemy in the flank, while Lt Starke in the SPW was to try to

Left: Easier days—the solar topee was issued universally, but worn less frequently as troops became acclimatised. Certainly it was of little use to the fighting troops, as it was extremely cumbersome and provided no protection from enemy fire. (*via TRH Pictures*)

enemy and to keep them occupied while the battalion carried out its various manoeuvres."

As the SPW moved off, Lt Starke opened fire, forcing the Americans to take cover. He also found the jeep, but it was empty. Lt Boy and the head of the column had now reached the main road and halted there. At this point Lt Starke came upon a company of 1st Panzer Regiment resting, and their commander "lent" him two tanks. With these and Lt Boy's company he advanced southwards down the track. The shooting had become widespread. Both sides were firing at each at point-blank range. The enemy appeared to be annoyed at having had their advance checked, but made little real attempt to break out of cover. It was only when Starke winkled them out of their scattered positions, by driving the SPW all over the place and firing at them with his machine gun, that the battalion could get forward and mount an attack and thus get to grips with them. The Germans soon had the situation under control.

"While Starke was doing this the enemy continually tried to knock out his SPW with bazookas, but did not succeed, and he could hardly believe his eyes at the number of enemy who continued to give themselves up. The engagement lasted into the afternoon by which time nearly 800 officers and men had surrendered, the majority being from an engineer battalion … The Americans were astounded at our small numbers—we were only a paltry 300 men—and they couldn't understand how we had captured them."

A further search of the area revealed the two Signal Platoon soldiers, both dead from wounds in the stomach—the only two deaths the battalion suffered that day. They

were laid out beside the American casualties on the main road.

They continued to make excellent progress: for example, the intrepid Lt Boy was sent to Kasserine with two light machine guns, one heavy machine gun and one anti-tank gun. Not only did he reach the pass and find it free of enemy but he also "let himself be entertained hospitably by the population, after which he swiftly returned!" Nevertheless, all received a universal order to halt that evening and the attack, which had promised so much, was allowed to peter out.

Following the eventual failure of the battle at and around Kasserine, which was retaken on the 25th, a weary Rommel turned to face Montgomery who was now preparing to assault the Mareth Line. This would, however, be Rommel's last battle in Africa, as he flew back to Germany to beg, unsuccessfully that his "Afrikans" be rescued. He was also not allowed to return to be with them at the end. Subsequently, Montgomery broke through, turning the end of the Mareth Line at El Hamma on 26 March, then successfully assaulting the final Axis position at Wadi Akarit on the night of 5/6 April.

By the middle of April, the Axis forces had been squeezed into a small perimeter in the hills around Tunis and Bizerta. They were heavily outnumbered—130 tanks and 500 guns opposed by 1,200 tanks and 1,500 guns—the end was inevitable. At 1200 hours on 12 May 1943, von Arnim capitulated.

THE END IN AFRICA

The most poignant surrender was of course that of the Deutsches Afrikakorps. Just before midnight on 12 May 1943, their

commander, General der Panzertruppe Hans Cramer, sent off this last signal:

"Ammunition shot off. Arms and equipment destroyed. In accordance with orders received the Afrikakorps has fought itself to the condition where it can fight no more. The Deutsches Afrikakorps must rise again. Heia Safari!"

ON TO SICILY & ITALY

From North Africa the victorious Allies went on to invade Sicily on 10 July 1943, in Operation Husky, the largest amphibious assault of the war apart from D-Day. The US Seventh (Patton) and British Eighth (Montgomery) Armies cleared the island by mid-August, despite determined and skillful German resistance.

This was followed almost immediately by the invasion of Italy—Operation Baytown—on 3 September when the British Eighth Army landed on the toe of Italy; then on 9 September, the US Fifth Army (Mark Clark) landed at Salerno (Operation Avalanche). There followed a long and drawn out campaign as the Germans fought another stubborn defensive battle all the way north, making maximum use of the mountainous country which runs up the "spine" of Italy. For some one and a half years of heavy fighting, they withdrew slowly from one fixed defensive line to the next—three of the main ones being the Hitler, Gustav and Gothic lines.

Despite the constant withdrawals, German morale stayed remarkably high, as did their fighting prowess. However, by the spring of 1945, the Allies had broken through the Gothic Line, captured the valley of the Po that lay beyond and the war in Italy was over.

Above Left: Dust clouds follow the withdrawal of the Afrikakorps. (*Colonel T. Bock*)

This Page: Scenes from Italy.
Above: On the lookout for enemy tanks, this infantryman is armed with a Haft-Holladung anti-tank mine.

Above Right: Generalfeldmarschall Dr Ing Wolfram Freiherr von Richthofen (in darker uniform) was in command of the Luftwaffe in the Mediterranean theatre.

Right: Infantry passing a heavy Elefant (also called Ferdinand) tank destroyer.

Below Right: In Italian mountain caves.

Below: Tired and unshaven in the act of surrendering; note DAK cuff title. (*All: Brian L. Davis Collection*)

Chapter 11 Northwest Europe

D-DAY

On 6 June 1944, the largest armada of ships in history landed the Allied invasion force on selected beaches in Normandy, having preceded these amphibious landings with an airborne assault on the previous night. D-Day had at last arrived, after months of planning and preparation that had begun in earnest once the United States entered the war. North Africa had been cleared and Sicily/Italy invaded. This delay had led to disagreements between the Allies and been accompanied throughout by continuous calls from the USSR to "Start a Second Front Now!" At last, the second front was a reality.

AIRBORNE LANDINGS

One of the many divisions facing the Allied invasion was the 711th Infantry Division, stationed between the Rivers Seine and Orne, with its headquarters at Pont-l'Eveque. Rommel had not been particularly impressed when he visited them in March 1944, caustically commenting that various of his orders did not seem to have percolated down to them so that they were "in ignorance of the concept of a land front. The foreshore has not yet been closed off with barriers."

In fact the 711th would find themselves initially facing an airborne threat during the night of 5–6 June, a threat that appeared to be landing very close to their divisional command post. Later, Generalleutnant Joseph Reichert, the divisional commander, recalled seeing several aircraft circling overhead, then saw some parachutes landing nearby and heard gunfire from the 20mm Flak guns that were deployed in the strongpoint. "Immediately after the alert had been given, the strongpoint was occupied by clerks, messengers, drivers, orderlies, etc. The guard company, which had been on duty hitherto, had had to be dissolved a few days before, to reinforce the front line troops." While one of his staff officers was

Above: This photograph was left behind in a dugout in the Cherbourg Peninsula and shows German soldiers in the area, prior to the invasion, wearing camouflage tunics made of string/net into which they could stick greenery. (Brian L. Davis Collection)

Left: German troops inspect an Allied glider which the caption says had been shot down during the Allied airborne assault on the night of 5/6 June, and crashlanded in the middle of their positions. Some of the occupants were killed and the rest were taken prisoner. (Brian L. Davis Collection)

rganising the defence of the strongpoint, Reichert ordered the alarm to be sent throughout his division, then sent a report to LXXXIst Army HQ at Rouen. "In the meantime," he recalled, "the first risoners—two parachutists who had anded in the strongpoint itself—were aken." No information was forthcoming from the prisoners, so the Germans did not now if a full-scale paratroop landing was oing to take place. However, things ventually quieted down and Reichert eckoned that this was probably a feint ttack, especially when reports came in that niformed straw dummies were being ropped—it was of course a ploy by the ritish to disguise the real airborne targets.

BLOODY OMAHA

There were real airborne landings that night on the flanks of the bridgehead area, designed to capture vital bridges, destroy gun positions, etc, but these were just a prelude to the main seaborne landings. Nowhere on all the five selected beaches was the fighting more severe than upon Omaha Beach, where US V Corps was spearheaded by America's senior infantry division—US 1st Infantry Division (the "Big Red One"). One of those opposing them was Untergefreiter Hein Severloh, who was manning a machine gun position. By midday he had fired over 12,000 rounds from his MG42 and down on the beach were the results—considerable numbers of dead men, each of whom had the figure "1" painted on their helmets. In fact by nightfall, over 1,000 GIs had been killed on "Bloody Omaha" and many more wounded. However, the German defences had not got off lightly. Within the strongpoint where Severloh was manning his machine gun, the mortar positions had been destroyed, the trenches had fallen in and many of the defenders had been killed. And despite their heavy casualties, instead of halting their attack, the enemy kept coming. Now they were unloading tanks. Tank shells began to arrive, one of the first penetrating directly through the viewing aperture of the OP (observation post) bunker. Then Severloh's machine gun was hit and badly damaged, losing its sights, while he received a shower of shell splinters in the face. He managed to continue to fire his weapon without its

broken sights by using the ammunition belts that had been filled for firing after dark and so had one tracer round in every five. This meant that he could watch the tracer in flight and alter his aim accordingly. Unfortunately, the enemy could also see his tracers and by following them back, pin-point his position. Quite soon a well-placed round from an off-shore destroyer practically obliterated the bunker. The tanks were now advancing over the beach, moving around to the flanks and plastering all the strongpoints with accurate, point-blank fire. It was time to leave. The artillery OP called for one last barrage and the infantry began to pull out from their wrecked positions, covering each other back off the beach and away to temporary safety. Throughout their withdrawal they were under a constant hail of fire, so that very few of them escaped unscathed. Severloh was one of the lucky ones and managed to get back to his battalion's battle headquarters, which was located between Coleville and the coast. Here he had the wounds to his face dressed and made his report.

THE NORMANDY CAMPAIGN & AFTER

Once established in the beachhead, the Allies sought to extend it, to include Caen in the east and Cherbourg in the west. The main thrust of the Allied plan was for the

British and Canadians in the east to draw the German armour into their sector, thus allowing US Third Army under General George S. Patton Jr. to break out on the Allied right. This was achieved and the advancing Allied armies had soon liberated most of France and significant portions of the Low Countries, while being joined by another equally successful landing of more forces in the South of France. All these successes forced the beleaguered Germans back even closer to the frontiers of the Fatherland. Nevertheless, they were not beaten yet.

As explained in the opening chapter, manpower problems had forced the Germans not only to extend the call-up to embrace all males between 16 and 60, but also to turn any available sailors and airmen into infantry. All these would serve in the newly formed Volksgrenadier divisions. Smaller, and with a lower scale of major weaponry, they would make up for some of their deficiencies with new weapons—such as the hand-held Panzerfaust and Panzerschreck in order to make up for a lack of anti-tank guns.

Hubert Gees was a young member of No 14 Company—infantry tank destroyers, operating in the Limburg area of Holland in September 1944. This is how he told his story to a Dutchman, Mr Ron van Rijt, at Heerlen, Holland in January 2000.

"An increasingly large number of German troops were withdrawing into Germany from the Western Front in the second half of August, 1944 ... I and my friend Abelius were due to attend reserve officers school at Aachen when we heard that the front line troops needed noncoms badly. I was ordered to go with Cadet Werner Bottcher as the second man of a Panzerschreck team [this was a two-man 8.8cm weapon, which was, to all intents and purposes, an

enlarged version of the American bazooka, and used the same principle. It could penetrate most Allied tanks and had a range of 150m]. My comrade Abelius formed a second tank destroyer team with another older soldier. After training we were attached to Infantry Battalion 464 at Eschweiler and on the morning of 4 September our group of 20–25 soldiers were marching up to the front from the German-Dutch border at Herzogenrath-Kerkrade into Dutch Limburg. We were supposed to help stop the fast approaching American Army—to 'scare' [the literal meaning of schreck] their tanks—but it scares me now when I think back about those days! However, we had plenty of guts back then! This may have been partly because of our youthful abandon—I was still only 17—but it was also because we were raised with the idea that it was our duty to do everything for the Fatherland.

"Several groups of Dutch civilians were standing behind their houses. They were probably discussing the latest news about the war. They surely knew about the fast-approaching front and were excited about the long-awaited liberation of their homeland. They surely must have wished us all to Hell—and out of their country. Maybe some of them even felt pity for us as Hitler's last 'gun-fodder'. But who can tell what people are thinking? We were standing on this side—the side on which we were almost born—and we had to do our duty as soldiers. We were not allowed to ask about the legality of this war. Completely one-sidedly informed, we believed the propaganda of our leaders, that right was on our side. 'Maybe I will have already experienced my baptism of fire by the time you read this letter'—that is what I hurriedly wrote to my parents in the early hours of 4 September.

"It was getting serious. The tension grew the more we went westwards. Our group had one or two machine guns. Werner Bottcher and myself 'organised' ourselves a bicycle (one flat tyre) on which we laid our 'stove pipe' [the Panzerschreck]. We also tied on two wooden boxes with four rockets in them so that we didn't have to carry everything, as we still each had a Panzerfaust [a smaller calibre one-man anti-tank weapon] on our shoulders. All together I'm sure we didn't look very frightening to the fully motorised American Army!

"The biggest danger for us in those days came from the sky. The American fighter planes—we called them 'Jabos'—attacked everything they recognised as enemy. That is when I realised that the twin-bodied Lightnings were not only shooting at us from the front when they attacked, but also from their rear when they pulled up again! The US Air Force had complete air supremacy and we very seldom saw our Luftwaffe.

"The first few days we went into position several times in the area of Wittem, Gulpen, Margraten and Valkenburg. Our main food consisted of mashed and cooked potatoes and apples—we called this food 'Heaven and Earth'. Around 7 or 8 September we were in position in a small field a few miles east of Maastricht, then in the afternoon we reached a big detached house. We piled up all the chairs and tables in a big room, then put straw on the floor to sleep on."

After spending a few days there, Hubert and his companions moved on, through Maastricht and out to the west side of the city, then on towards the Dutch-Belgian border, eventually coming to the canal.

"Our staff went into a big farmhouse on the right side of the road. The road over the

Left: One of the most useful weapons in the infantryman's arsenal was the stick grenade (*Stielgranate 24*) which had up to a 4.5-second-delay fuse, which this rifleman is altering. (*Brian L Davis Collection*)

Right: Allied air superiority in northwest Europe and Italy meant that anti-aircraft defence became a prerequisite for German military units, who also became very adept at camouflage and movement at night. (*via TRH Pictures*)

Above: The backbone of the army. A typical infantryman removes his "coal scuttle" helmet during a welcome breather from the battle. His matted hair and beads of perspiration show his exhaustion. (*Brian L. Davis Collection*)

Above Right: Smoke break. Some battle-stained troops stop for a quick smoke. (*Brian L. Davis Collection*)

Far Right: An MG34 team, using their machine gun in the light role on its bipod. Its rate of fire (8-900rpm) was nearly twice that of the British Bren gun. (*Brian L. Davis Collection*)

Albert Canal into Belgium was at the end of the row of border houses on the left side of the road. The steel bridge was blasted—its front part was lying in the water and its rear part was pointing to the sky. On the left side in front of this demolished bridge we quickly dug a long trench in a zigzag line. We got some doors out of the houses at the border to put over our trench, then covered them with a lot of soil for better protection. We discovered how much we would need this trench within the next few days. The American recce plane—we called it the 'Crow'—came in from a southwesterly direction. One of our machine guns fired at it, but then the American artillery gave us our 'baptism of fire' right away—this made us much more careful in the following days … Thanks to our good trench no one got wounded, although our trench was destroyed in a few places.

"At our command post at the big farmhouse, where we had our field kitchen, a small accident happened. I was showing one of our comrades how to use a Panzerfaust and had the head of the weapon in one hand and was explaining how it worked and where the safety pin was in the long tube. I pressed the firing button (to show that the safety pin worked) there was a loud explosion and a lot of smoke—the safety catch had failed and the weapon exploded! Our men rushed out of the farmhouse to see what had happened, but, except for a few blisters on my left hand, I was OK— Thank God!

"We arrived at the Albert Canal on 9 September and one week later, in the early morning of the 16th, we received

orders to retreat quickly to the north. If remember correctly, we crossed a swing bridge, then crossed the River Meuse in rubber boats at the north side of Maastrich and before noon we reached a town called Bunde, some six miles north of Maastricht At the centre of the town, not far from the church, some troops were teaching a few others how to use the Panzerschreck . These men were wearing gasmasks because of the backblast while firing. They were all very glad when we arrived as we were already trained on how to destroy tanks during close combat. We took over their weapons as ours were still in a lorry that had yet to cross the river.

"What was the reason for our fas retreat on the morning of 16 September. The Americans had broken through Maastricht from a southeasterly direction on the 14th without us even noticing it, a we were on the western side of the city, so we had to retreat quickly to prevent getting encircled. On the 16th, just after we had taken over the 'stove pipes' we received a tank alarm! American tanks were approaching along the main road from Maastricht to the north—these were the tanks of the 2nd Armored Division.

"We quickly started to dig in behind hedge along the main road about a mile east of Bunde at the little hamlet of Kasen Abelius and I, both second men on the Panzerschreck and responsible fo ammunition, quickly ran into Bunde to ge some more rockets. We had not go completely back to our positions, when an American tank came into view, moved into a garden with an orchard and began firing its machine gun at the hedge where we

were lying in a shallow ditch. Tracer bullets were flying over us as we pressed our bodies into the bottom of the ditch. Artillery rounds began exploding in the fields behind us. Fighter planes were also attacking targets on the ground. Wounded started screaming. At this moment I thought, 'This is the end!'

"Suddenly the tank that was firing at us drove behind a small patch of trees and stopped firing for a moment. We both thought, 'it's now or never!' If the tank appeared on the other side of the small patch of trees then he would immediately see us lying behind the hedge and that would mean the end of our lives! So we used this last chance. Both of us jumped up and started to run in the direction of Kasen and Bunde. We stormed straight through a hedge of thorns—steel helmet first!—just before the tank appeared on the other side of the trees. A pile of manure gave us some shelter. Then we retreated slowly, hiding under some big fruit trees.

"It was of no importance that I lost my gasmask in front of the hedge, but I never saw my No 1 on the Panzerschreck team, Werner Bottcher, ever again. Later, my parents showed me two letters they had received from his father when I came home from POW camp in 1947. In the first, written in December 1944, he asked if they had received any news from me; the second was written in 1946 and said that they had just received news that he was dead."

Hubert Gees would manage to rejoin the remnants of his sub-unit on the 17th and the company was next attached to the Fusilier battalion of the 275th Infantry Division. They went into a defensive line just south of Scherpenseel, but did not stay there long as they driven out by more American tanks. Fortunately the tanks then followed the paved road, so they were able to withdraw safely, regroup and take up another defensive position, only for it to happen all over again, with their division involved in heavy fighting all the time. Hubert concludes this part of his narrative:

"On 28 November, the remnants of our company and our beaten Fusilier battalion were taken prisoner by the Americans when we lost the village of Hürtgen. In the American archives it is written that only seven men of our company remained."

IN THE HÜRTGEN FOREST

"We were transported from our training camp at Doberitz to Kall at Gemund in the Eifel, via Magdeburg, Kreiensen, Hoxter, Soest and Neuss, arriving there on 4 November 1944. Because of the cloudy November weather there were no enemy fighters or reconnaissance aircraft. But we could clearly hear the artillery fire as we got nearer to the front line—we were back at war again!"

Otto Gunkel of 272 VGD was going back to the front after his unit had been reformed and retrained as a Volksgrenadier division.

"After unloading we marched in a long column, through Gemund and uphill via Herhahn, to Einruhr in the Ruhr valley, then later, on to Hofen, to take over the prepared positions of the 89th Infantry Division.

"Our arrival at the front and the movement of our troops did not go unnoticed by the enemy—Americans this time—and during the night they hammered our sector with artillery. We were manning pillboxes on the German-Belgian border. As a runner I was out most of the day with our company commander, checking the front lines. We found good cover here because of the forest. We could see the little village of Monschau that the Americans had already occupied, and we could see their infantry positions on the high plains across the border. There were several small engagements and we got used to the front again, without any losses. Then the 980th Regiment took over our positions and we were switched to take over to man other positions to the north of Simmerath, in the centre of our divisional sector in the area from Kall-Schleiden-Hofen on the left, then Heimbach-Schmidt-Vossenack on the right. We would stay in this area until the end of February 1945. During this entire time we were always within easy reach of enemy artillery and could never feel secure, no matter what we were doing.

"The relief took place in pouring rain and the dark. It was difficult because of the bad forest tracks in the strange area and especially because of the continuous incoming artillery. Soaking wet and tired we arrived at Einruhr and the next day we were attacked by American Lightnings—we could remember them well from Normandy! A lot of artillery shelling followed, as we prepared to march off that evening and our *company had its first losses of men and horses. Company HQ lost its runner, Leonard, hit by shrapnel.*

"During the night we reached Eicherscheidt by way of Rauchenauel, Dedenborn and Hammer and went into a pillbox at the edge of the village. This was a communications pillbox manned by men of our 8th Company plus the men of the communications unit. Because of the importance of continuous communications, the telephone wires had to be checked day and night and the runners had to do this work. So I had a crash course and then went out repairing the broken wires, especially at night. It was a dangerous and exhausting job.

"Battalion HQ was inside another pillbox at the other end of the village and our three companies were positioned in pillboxes and trenches along the border road, which ran from Aachen to Monschau, via the villages of Simmerath and Imgenbroich. Our heavy machine guns, howitzers and mortars were positioned in and around Eicherscheidt and Huppenbroich. All these defensive positions were connected by telephone, partly the ground wire of the Siegfried Line and partly newly laid field wire, which was often destroyed by enemy artillery fire. We always sent two men to repair the breaks. This was extremely difficult on the dark November nights, because the wire was often blown away quite a distance and sometimes broken in several places. We needed to crawl on hands and knees in a circle of some 50 plus yards looking for the broken ends. We had to do this every night, sometimes up to six times a night in the dark and rain!

"Fortunately there wasn't much fighting. Tanks and heavy weapons were almost impossible to move in the hilly landscape. The static war lasted for about three weeks. Life in the cold, wet pillboxes wasn't very comfortable—but at least we were safe behind those thick concrete walls! Then the first snows came in mid-November. We could hear the noisy V-1 rockets flying overhead in the direction of Antwerp and London from 16 November onwards—this was the new wonder-weapon that Goebbels told us would bring victory.

"While it stayed fairly quiet in our sector, the Americans built up their strength as they planned to break through from the Aachen-Stolberg area towards Duren, then on to reach the Cologne plain and the Rhine. This fight raged in the forested area around Hürtgen–Bergstein–Vossenack. The fighting in the Hürtgen Forest would go on for many weeks and the area would get a sad and bloody name in history.

"On 27 November, our regiment was sent to support the hard-pressed 89th Infantry Division, taking up positions

between Birgel and Gey. We found holding trenches in the open very difficult after weeks in the dry pillboxes, especially as we were short of winter clothing. The melting slush and rain lasted for days, turning the soil into a quagmire and filling our trenches with mud. We looked like pigs after a few days! It made us shudder to think about the coming winter months, in which we would have to struggle to survive.

"On 2 December the Americans broke through our defences in several places and we had to counterattack to restore our lines. 1st Battalion advanced at first light in the direction of the Hubertus hills and our 2nd Battalion attacked Gey after an artillery barrage and with the support of our assault guns. We started to push them back, but then their resistance stiffened and our attack broke down. We had to dig a new

defensive line under heavy enemy fire. Our companies dug in on both sides of the road uphill from Gey to Kleinhau and Hürtgen, with our heavy machine guns behind them at the edge of the village of Gey. The company command post was in a cellar at the crossroads, our mortars in the hedges behind Gey and our howitzers at Horm. We held these positions for the next seven days. It was a horrible position because the Americans could look right into our lines from the edge of the forest on the hills outside Gey. The enemy artillery observers could see our every move and they threw more artillery and mortar fire at us than ever before. They even used phosphorous to smoke us out—a really nasty thing. NCO Kohler was wounded on the first day—he had been with us since Normandy, then Jaeckel, Kroll and Emmerich, while they

Left: Two despatch riders in their issue waterproof coats (a very practical double-breasted, rubberised and loose-fitting garment) enjoy a cigarette. Note also their issue goggles. (*via TRH Pictures*)

Far Left: A *General der Infanterie* commanding one of the operational divisions, visits a front line battle group and talks to one of his commanders, 15 July 1944. (*Brian L. Davis Collection*)

Drove, Soller, Thum and on to Vlatten. This was all that was left of the 2nd Battalion of the 981st Regiment—only one-third of its strength. Our company HQ detachment was only four men. Both our heavy machine gun platoons were down to squad size. No 5 Company had been wiped out—dead, wounded or taken prisoner. That was the horrible result of only 10 days in the Hürtgen Forest, even worse than the first 10 days in Normandy. The battalion never recovered from these losses until it was disbanded in March 1945. A few replacements just could not make up for our lack of men. I walked behind the horse-drawn cart loaded with our dead of the day before—Walter Eckhardt was among them.

"We buried them the same day in the cemetery of Vlatten, beside the church, but today they are buried in the German war cemetery at Gemund/Eifel.

"That same night we were going to march down the road to Gemund, to spend a few days resting while waiting for reinforcements. Instead we received new orders—the regiment was to take over positions at Simmerath and Huppenbroich immediately. We couldn't understand this, because the woods and small villages around Gemund were full of soldiers from newly arrived units. These men were well equipped with winter camouflage uniforms, winter boots, fur-hoods, etc, etc. Long convoys of armoured vehicles, assault guns and artillery were blocking all the roads. What we didn't know was that these troops were getting ready for the great Ardennes Offensive that would start on 16 December and was meant to turn the tide of war for Germany!"

were out working on the telephone wires. One of our mortar crews was wiped out by a direct hit. Three more of my comrades were killed while they tried to rescue others in no-man's land. And so it went on. In ten days the battalion lost 194 men (killed, wounded and missing), so that by 6 December we had only 164 men left. I was wounded again by shrapnel—above my right knee, but it wasn't serious enough to put me into hospital. After some first aid treatment I went back to my comrades.

"During the night of the 10th I spent hours outside as a runner with the company commander. We visited all our positions to warn them of another attack, and did not get back to our cellar until gone 2am. I talked for a while to Walter Eckhardt, who was also a runner and an old friend. He took over duty in the CP and

I went to sleep in the corner of the cellar. It would be our last conversation as he was hit in the chest by shrapnel while taking a message to one of the mortar positions.

"The enemy attack took place in the early morning. The Americans pushed through our thin defensive line and got into the village. There was house to house fighting—we fought man to man. Sgt Holler, two others and myself managed to overrun a group of Americans in Brown Farm and took them prisoner. We locked them in the cellar to make it easier to guard them. Our situation became more precarious that day, but then we received reinforcements and that night some units of 89th Infantry Division relieved us.

"A sad little group of tired soldiers, dirty, unshaven and in torn uniforms, we marched upstream through Kreuzau,

Above: The 5cm leichte Granatwerfer 36 was the standard light mortar in the early years of the war (see photograph on page 27), but made its appearance again with second-line and reserve units as they joined in the battles in defence of the Reich. It had a maximum range of 520m. (*Brian L. Davis Collection*)

Above Right: Anti-tank gunners engaging enemy tanks in the fighting around Falaise. The 7.5cm Pak 40 provided heavy antitank capability allied to a low silhouette, although it lost something in manoeuverability because of its weight. (*James Lucas*)

THE ARDENNES OFFENSIVE

Deliberately codenamed *Wacht am Rhein* (Watch on the Rhine) to disguise its true intention, this audacious German counter thrust, which began on 16 December 1944, was directed against a seemingly quiet area of the American sector, between Echternach and Monschau, which was held by just six divisions of the US V and VIII Corps containing green or exhausted troops.

Leutnant Horst Lück was in command of the 2nd Battalion of the 89th Grenadier Regiment in the 12th Volksgrenadier Division (VGD), which had been rebuilt in the early autumn of 1944 to nearly 15,000 men. It had been sent to the Aachen area in mid-September, then would fight as part of I SS Panzer Corps during the Ardennes offensive. As he recalled to Mr Ron van Rijt:

"Our stay in Losheimergraben as a reserve lasted only for a short period. It was said that because the 48th Grenadier Regiment could not advance fast enough at Murringen, that the 1st Battalion of the 89th Grenadier Regiment was sent in.

However, they received heavy losses during the attack on 17 December, so my 2nd Battalion of the 89th Grenadier Regiment came earlier into battle than expected. We advanced between Murringen and Hunningen on the 18th. On the right side of Bullingen there were some RAD barracks in the forest. We were able to surround some enemy troops there and took about 80 prisoners, but most importantly also some Jeeps, plus all kinds of supplies and weapons. Some trucks had been destroyed and others were disappearing in the direction of Bullingen. I asked for artillery fire on Bullingen, but our artillery were still on the move. We sent off some disarmed GIs with a few of their wounded to the units behind our front lines. Then another unit on our left attacked Bullingen, while we made a fighting reconnaissance of the Bullingen railway track and dam, with some of the captured jeeps and wearing American coats. We received enemy fire and asked for the support of our infantry guns. The Americans had to retreat because the unit next to us pushed through as well, while we put in a two-company flank attack. Our neighbouring unit took Bullingen that evening and we held the

106

right-hand edge of the village. We used Panzerfaust against three cellars to force stubborn enemy to surrender, then we prepared to defend our position during the night, well supplied with American rations.

"That evening we received orders that the battalion had to attack and take Wirtzfeld. I discussed the plan and the supply of weapons with my company commanders. I ordered two companies to attack in an encircling move, keeping the machine guns of both companies in the middle sector in support. The third company would be in reserve and would bring up the jeeps, captured weapons and ammunition—and all that great food! As it turned out, the loss of the important Bullingen crossroads and railway had such an impact on the Americans that we were able to take Wirtzfeld without artillery or tank support.

"When we advanced along the main road, the Americans left most of their supplies behind in their hurry to get out of the village. Our encircling move and the covering of the road with our machine guns worked out as planned.

"One thing I must mention, we found one of our V-1 rockets in a stable when we searched the village. It had come down but had failed to explode.

"We took about 70 prisoners, whom we sent back with a jeep to transport their wounded and some of ours—the jeep would also bring back some ammunition for us. This jeep did, in fact, come back before evening with some ammunition, and it even brought some supply vehicles with it. We were lucky about that, because we found out the next morning that we were cut off from our own supply unit.

"I sent a message to the regiment to tell them that Wirtzfeld was taken. Orders came back that our positions must be defended at all costs, because the other battalion had still not taken the positions on our right at Krinkelt. I then needed to take my most important decision of the war—it would also prove to be my most correct order of the war as well! Of course I would have preferred to have a rest in a cellar!

"I talked over the situation with my company commanders and decided to order everyone in the battalion less our reserve company, to take up positions on the northern and western sides of the village. The 3rd (Reserve) Company, which had only suffered a few casualties, had to

defend our right flank. They also had to bring up all the gear that the Americans had left on the north side of the village. In addition, each company had to bring its supplies from the south side of the village to the north side. We dug in, prepared our defensive positions, dug machine gun nests, camouflaged the entrances to these positions, and we had our 'quarters' only in the cellars. We never worked so hard as on this day, and fortunately were not disturbed by the enemy.

"Then I issued a strict order that no-one must go in the southern part of the village from 20 December onwards. Each company also had to position one platoon (they weren't that big any more during those days) further behind them in the cellars—they would be our reserve. The Battalion Command Post was in a cellar of a white house in the middle of our sector, right in the front line. Every two-man position or foxhole had twice as many weapons as normal because of all the enemy weapons we had captured.

"From the 21st onwards we noticed that it was GIs of the 2nd Infantry Division who were in the Elsenborn area and had artillery in position in this sector. We

couldn't go into the southern sector of the village any more. I guess we were lucky to have a lake and a dam on our left side, because we didn't get any trouble from American tanks.

"After that I had the first of my daily walks along the front line, undisturbed, then we had terrific German/American food and slept until we were relieved. This was the quietest night of the six nights that would follow. It was still quiet during the morning and again I checked our front-line positions. We were told to hold our village come what may—the 'easy time' would be over soon. In the afternoon we received our first enemy artillery shells, in the centre of the village and far behind our lines—the rounds rumbled over our heads. Preparations for their first attack that evening. Our lines held and the Americans retreated. We found that we had to improve our defensive positions some more. We also had to get information about the enemy positions, so I sent out small reconnaissance patrols. I knew that the Americans usually attacked as follows: a long massed artillery preparation, tank attacks to destroy enemy resistance, then the infantry. We were lucky that tanks could not be used at all in our area, but there was loads of artillery. Fortunately because our infantry and theirs were lying very close to each other, most of the rounds landed behind our lines. Only once did their artillery put their fire close to our lines, and that time they hit more of their own troops than they did ours—then it was quiet again.

"My order: 'Every man and weapon to the forward edge of the village' had clearly been the right order. Then I gave the companies orders on the 22nd to get as many men as possible into their defensive positions. There was only a small enemy artillery barrage. And then, against all the 'rules', the Americans put in a much stronger infantry attack right across the hill—taking in almost our whole battalion sector. My orders had been to let them come as close as possible, so thanks to our tremendous firepower, the attack was broken up in a horrible way. Now their artillery came down again, but in the centre and lower part of the village. Our own artillery couldn't be used as the enemy was just too close... The rest of the American infantry retreated, their artillery still firing behind our lines. Then silence—broken only by cries for help from wounded GIs.

"After half an hour we saw an American soldier with a Red Cross flag and two officers behind him on top of the hill. I sent runners to my company command posts—'Cease Fire!' Then I went with an orderly officer and a runner to the three Americans. I didn't know what rank the Americans were, but they surely outranked me! We saluted each other, then they asked for a cease-fire of an hour to get their dead and wounded out of the front line.

"Later these American officers would come back and the same thing would happen again. The talking was mainly in English although one of the officers could speak a little German— this time there was an exchange of cigarettes 'Camel' and 'Attika', a shake of hands and a salute before both sides went back to their positions.

"On 23 December the American artillery completely cut off our supplies. Suddenly at about 1400 hours another

Above: Field telephones with landlines were widely used as they were far more secure than wireless; however, as the narrative tells, they were liable to damage from shell fire. (Brian L. Davis Collection)

Right: This infantryman is carrying an MG34 over his shoulder, butt-first. (via TRH Pictures)

enemy infantry attack. The motto was sti 'let them come close'. This time the firin increased with every gun we had. Th American attack wasn't along the entir sector, instead it focussed on the mos forward White House—where we had ou Battalion Command Post in the cellar, bu the Americans could not have known this We never found out what it looked like o the first floor because during the day ther were snipers and during the dark we couldn't use any lights! We had a enormous number of weapons, while ou machine gun platoons were firing from th flanks. Although this attack was eve stronger than the last one, it was pushe back by our firepower, though there wer tremendous losses on both sides. I fought fo over three years in Russia and experience massive Russian infantry attacks there, bu I never experienced such a concentrate attack as this one. For three-quarters of a hour it went on and on, then we knew wha would happen—another 'shake hands', a exchange of cigarettes and a shor conversation. The senior American office

gave me his card. He said that if I should become a POW, or later, after the war, I should use this card. Later when I was taken prisoner and was lying in hospital, the card and a pocketknife were taken by an American doctor—I feared that they would think that I had stolen the card.

"The American officer expressed his respect for our brave soldiers and said: 'Christmas is for both of us a holy, beautiful happening. You can celebrate Christmas undisturbed, because there won't be any attack on 24 or 25 December and no artillery will be fired.' This promise was kept. We almost couldn't believe it, but we celebrated Christmas peacefully with all the food that we had captured earlier. This was how the pause was accomplished that is mentioned in the Hans Zeplien report—this was my battalion of the 89th Grenadier Regiment. The road to Wirtzfeld in our battalion sector always seemed pretty strongly protected in my opinion—a good thing that we prepared our well-placed defensive positions properly on the first day.

"We kept our positions on the heights northwest of Wirtzfeld without too many losses. Then on the night of 25–26 December we heard the sound of tracked vehicles coming from behind us—it was an armoured reconnaissance car and another vehicle from Regimental HQ. Our sentries brought two officers into the cellar. They were surprised to see us in such good shape, because they hadn't had any messages from us since our dispatch rider had been killed. After we had drunk a bottle of red wine, we toured our positions because the Hauptmann had been sent to relieve me. I went back to RHQ and reported that my battalion was still there and in good shape. Then I slept for a while.

"I still have my military passbook with my awards written inside. Beside mentioning that I was awarded the Golden Honour Leaf Medal for bravery and my award for being wounded eight times, it ends with my last leave: 'relief for bravery, it says, 'from 26 December 1944 to 19 January 1945,'" and I was able to spend it in my homeland, on the other side of the River Oder at Lansberg, Warthe.

Above: An infantry section, complete with MG42, passes a PzKpfw V Panther, probably the finest medium-heavy tank of the war. They may be "marrying-up" with the tanks for a tank/infantry operation. (Brian L. Davis Collection)

"When I got back around the 20th I found that only some parts of our supply unit and my loyal runner Alfred Braun were still there. He told me that the battalion had attacked towards St Vith-Bastogne. Then around 6 January, the Americans had broken through and the 2nd Battalion of the 89th Grenadier Regiment had been annihilated or taken prisoner. About 23 January, they started to rebuild the battalion at Dueren. The terrific young sailors went for the first time into the field behind the front line and were trained as infantry ... then we went to the Eifel to try to slow down the American attack and I was wounded."

Chapter 12 Disaster in the East

IN THE STALINGRAD POCKET

The capture of Stalingrad had, by late September 1942, assumed an importance to both sides out of all proportion to its actual strategic importance, although General Zhukov had appreciated that its capture would allow the Germans to cut off the south of the country. In addition, of course, Stalin was determined that the city that bore his name would never be taken. So it became the "Verdun" of World War II. Then the tables were turned and the Russians began a counter-offensive which, by November, had successfully bottled up 20 enemy divisions under General von Paulus, so that now the erstwhile attacker had become the beleaguered, with the Germans trying desperately to get a relief column through. They were unsuccessful, even though von Manstein got to within 35 miles in December. Hitler would not let von Paulus's embattled Sixth Army break out and by mid-January 1943, they had been squeezed into a small pocket with a diameter of just over 20 miles. On 31 January, von Paulus, with his remaining 90,000 troops surrendered after more than 200,000

Germans had been killed or died in the bitter winter weather. Undoubtedly it was one of the major turning points of the war.

One of the units caught in this trap was the 2nd Battalion of the 132nd Infantry Regiment, whose last hours were graphically recounted in the US Army pamphlet *Small Unit Actions*:

"The life expectancy of the encircled Sixth Army depended upon its ability to defend the perimeter. If the Russians succeeded in breaking through the German ring at any point, they would split the encircled army into smaller pockets, capture the remaining airfields, and thus cut off supply by air. Ration and ammunition dumps would fall into their hands and the German resistance would crumble. Although sporadic fighting might continue, such isolated German resistance would merely have nuisance value and could be eliminated in the course of mopping-up operations.

"This explains the ferocity with which both sides fought to force a decision. The stakes were high and the Germans needed cool-headed leaders. Whereas German unit commanders could envisage the possibility of a voluntary withdrawal during the first and second phases of the encirclement,

static, positional defence was mandatory during the third. At this stage, Russian front-line propaganda took over. On New Year's Day Russian psychological warfare teams went to work. Night after night loudspeakers blared forth speeches by German refugees from a studio in Moscow, who read appeals, ostensibly from German mothers and wives, imploring their loved ones to give up the fight. German prisoners, who had been confined in model Russian camps, were sent back across the lines to their former units to report the excellent treatment they had received.

"The prospect of relief from the outside had meanwhile grown dimmer. Nevertheless, the men in the pocket refused to give up hope, even if there was every indication that the Sixth Army was doomed. Living conditions in the pocket went from bad to worse. The German infantrymen had to stay in their foxholes exposed to snow and rain, extreme cold and sudden thaw. Again and again the

Below: A 334th Infantry Division ski patrol near Jekimowo, March 1942. (*Hans Unhold*)

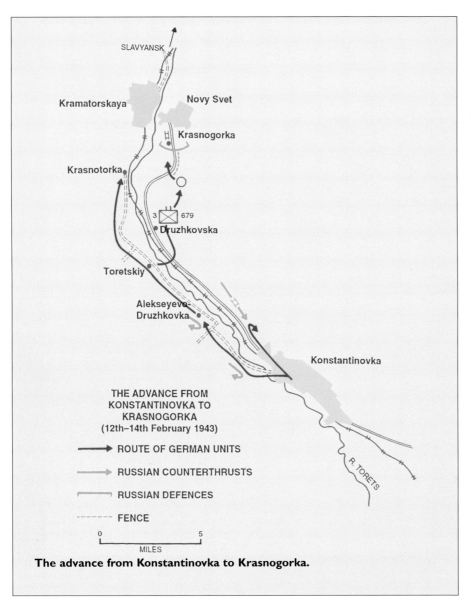

SLAVYANSK

Kramatorskaya

Novy Svet

Krasnogorka

Krasnotorka

3 ◻ 679
Druzhkovska

Toretskiy

Alekseyevo-
Druzhkovka

Konstantinovka

R. TORETS

THE ADVANCE FROM
KONSTANTINOVKA TO
KRASNOGORKA
(12th–14th February 1943)

➤ ROUTE OF GERMAN UNITS

➤ RUSSIAN COUNTERTHRUSTS

RUSSIAN DEFENCES

FENCE

0 ————— 5
MILES

The advance from Konstantinovka to Krasnogorka.

launch an immediate thrust northward towards Kramastorskaya. The battalion assembled and their advance guard immediately began to move off. However at 0800 hours their point ran into a Russian tank force and was annihilated, the advance guard routed and the main body which was just moving out of the railhead was seized with an acute case of what can only be described as "tank jitters!" The account tells how:

"*The regimental commander realised that he had to act immediately. Fear of tanks had gripped the battalion, turning gallant soldiers into quivering cowards. What could he do? The overall situation was none too favourable since the 2nd Battalion was not due to arrive for 12 hours and the 1st Battalion would take at least another 24.*

"*When he discovered that a self propelled gun was undergoing repair in the rail head, he commandeered it immediately. Realising that the danger of encountering enemy tanks was greatest to the east of the River Torets he chose the road running along the west bank as the new axis of advance.*

"*The regimental and battalion commanders mounted the assault gun and proceeded to lead the advance northwards. The men were heartened by the sight of their two commanders speeding northward along the new route without encountering any opposition. They quickly regained their confidence and, falling in behind their leaders, moved forward with new courage. Against light opposition, the battalion fought its way to Alekseyevo-Druzhkovka and during the night, the newly arrived 2nd Battalion closed up and moved into the same town.*

"*On the 13th, as a result of the previous day's experience, the regimental commander decided to employ the 2nd Battalion as the leading element in order to condition the unit to combat in Russia. To simulate greater strength all motorised vehicles were ordered to follow the leading battalion in plain view of the enemy. The deception could only be used because enemy interference from the air was not expected.*

"*Towards evening the 2nd Battalion arrived in Krasnotorka without major incident. During the night, however, the battalion suffered heavy casualties from frostbite when the battalion commander who was unfamiliar with the severe winter weather, ordered sentries to be posted in the open outside the village. The deception, however, had been successful judging by an intercepted Russian radio message in which the enemy commander was warned that strong German motorised formations were advancing toward Kramastorskaya.*

rations were cut. At first every man was issued with one third of a loaf of bread per day, then a quarter and later a fifth. This monotonous diet was occasionally supplemented by a few slices of sausage and a meat broth obtained by boiling horse meat. Only the wounded were given half a bar of chocolate and some brandy immediately after evacuation to revive their spirits.

"*Constant Russian pressure resulted in a steadily growing number of casualties. The 2nd Battalion's combat strength diminished gradually. When the Russians resumed their large-scale attacks early in January, 1943, the battalion had only three officers and 160 men left. In mid-January, the executive officer was killed in close combat during a counterattack. On the following day the battalion commander committed suicide as the result of a nervous breakdown. On 19 January, the battalion's last remaining officer, a platoon commander of Company G, launched a final desperate counterthrust and led the last 13 men of the battalion to their deaths. A few days later, at the beginning of*

February 1943, the battle of Stalingrad came to an end.*"

After liquidating the Stalingrad pocket, the Russians launched a powerful offensive westwards. It was virtually unstoppable as there just were not any German operational units left in the sector, so, by the beginning of February they had reached Slavyansk. In an effort to stem the tide, XL Panzer Corps (consisting of two Panzer and one infantry divisions) was moved up from the south and ordered to drive the Russians back across the Donets River. The winter weather was typical, with deep snow covering everywhere and temperatures that reached -49°F at night. Such conditions were enough to sap the resolve and hardiness of the most optimistic German soldier!

The 679th Infantry Regiment of the 333rd Infantry Division, which was the infantry division of XL Panzer Corps, had never previously seen combat in Russia. They were moved up to the railhead at Konstantivoka, the leading battalion (3rd Battalion) detraining at 0400 hours on 12 February, when they received orders to

Left: Horse-drawn sledges parked outside a farmhouse, near Smolensk. (*H-G. Sandmann*)

Below Left and Below: After the battle—an evocative photograph of an machine gun position with an MG34, "potato masher" grenades, and a welter of expended cartridge cases ... and the results of the accurate machine gun fire still visible. (*H-G. Sandmann*)

"*The regimental commander moved the 1st Battalion, the last one to arrive, to Toretskiy with orders to capture Krasnogorka the next day. At dawn the 1st Battalion crossed the river, passed through Druzhkovka and moved into a hollow about two miles south of Krasnogorka. The cross-country march in deep snow was exhausting because the motorised equipment constantly bogged down and had to be pulled out by wreckers. Nevertheless, the battalion had reached its start line by 1000 hours.*

"*The situation facing the battalion commander was exasperating. Ahead of him lay the strongly defended Krasnogorka, from where a few enemy tanks were firing in his direction. Between him and his objective, lay a vast expanse of snow that was more than three feet deep. Despite the promised support from a medium artillery battery, a direct frontal assault on the town was bound to fail and involve heavy casualties. From afar, the Russians could observe the individual German soldiers cautiously inching their way forward, their silhouettes clearly outlined against the* white background and could pick them off at will. Although the regimental commander shared his apprehensions, the attack had to be launched and Krasnogorka captured.

"*The only landmark that broke the monotony of the flat landscape was a high, snow-covered fence extending for about two miles along the right side of the road from the turning to the village. This fence, which looked more like a wall of snow, might conceal the troops while they worked their way forward towards the objective in single file, hugging the fence. Although this was far from being an ideal solution, it was the only apparent way out. To deceive the Russian garrison and divert its attention, one company was to be echeloned in depth and would advance on a wide front on the left side of the road. While this company was launching its diversionary attack, the rest of the battalion crept along to within 500 yards of the objective. The Russians fell for this ruse and concentrated the fire of their multi-barrelled rocket launchers, self-propelled guns and mortars on the single company, which was promptly* pinned down. Meanwhile the main assault force infiltrated Krasnogorka and seized it in short order. Because of the deep snow the Battalion took two hours to cover the two mile stretch along the fence. The Russians were taken completely by surprise and beat a hasty retreat to Kramatorskaya. A few days later, the regiment, committed as a unit for the first time, followed up this initial success by seizing Slavyansk after overcoming stiff Russian resistance.*"

Undoubtedly the regimental commander made some decisions that must have been at variance with accepted practice—such as mounting on the assault gun and leading the column, or sending his main attack force along a one soldier front. He also had a good deal of luck. However, through his flair and quick thinking, he had turned a dispirited unit with a lowering morale into an aggressive one. Nevertheless, even with such quick-thinking commanders, the writing was on the wall for the Germans and they would soon be forced to withdraw farther and farther westwards.

FIGHTING FOR BERLIN

The last months of the war saw the German Army disintegrating, despite its considerable strength—the last OKW return showed nearly four million men under arms, but they were being pushed back on every front. In the west, after the failure of the Ardennes offensive, the Americans, British and Canadians entered Germany, crossed the Rhine and drove into the very heart of the Fatherland. In the east, the Soviets continued their unrelenting pressure, thrusting into Poland, clearing the Baltic States and the Balkans, driving on to the Oder and then on into East Germany, until by April, they were at the gates of Berlin. Now the youngsters of the Hitler Youth joined in, together with the elderly, both as reinforcements and as ad hoc defenders. The older teenagers—16 and 17-year olds who had received some military training, were sent to join units on the outskirts and beyond, even as far as the Oder and the Niesse, to fight off the oncoming Red Army, while the younger ones—some even as young as 10—were held back, ready to fight for their city in the rubble-strewn streets against the Russian tanks and battle-hardened infantry, the men whom the Germans had despised as being *Untermensch* (subhuman). Most of them were now bent on wreaking a terrible vengeance on the people of Berlin.

One such 17-year old was Helmuth Altner. He had been in the Heer for just three weeks, when he found himself being sent to guard the village of Lietzen. It was first light on 16 April 1945 and the Russians were just 12 km away on the Oder River front and he could clearly hear the sounds of battle, the roar of the guns, the clouds of dense black smoke as yet another building was destroyed. After the war, he described his experiences in *Totentanz, Berlin*, telling how the village that lay behind him was being shelled, while handfuls of refugees trudged wearily past. He had been left on the road at the eastern approaches to the village as a lookout, with an even younger companion—his friend Stroschn—while the rest of his sub-unit went to pick up new weapons from their battalion headquarters in the village. The shelling had stopped for a while, but the village had "been damaged beyond all recognition. Some farmers were trying to rescue cattle from blazing sheds, while other distraught villagers sought missing relations. The smell of scorched flesh hung heavily over the shattered buildings."

Then their new weapons were distributed. Altner was very pleased to receive an Italian sub-machine gun (probably a Moschetto automatico modello 38/42 that was produced for both Italian and German units), discovering how to fire it only when he nearly shot himself in the foot! The two boys then ran back to the village and almost died of fright when a massive German railway gun near the village began firing. However, it was destroyed in a bombing raid soon afterwards. By midday, the bombing and shelling had had the inevitable result and Altner's unit began to take casualties. Notwithstanding this blow to his morale, his belief in final victory was given a boost by a new Führer Order which read:

"Berlin stays German, Vienna will be German again and Europe will never become Russian. Form yourselves into sworn brotherhoods to defend not only the concept of the Fatherland, but your homes, your wives, your children and, with them, our future. In these hours the entire German people look to you, my eastern warriors, and only hope that by your resolve, your determination, your weapons and under your leadership, the Bolshevik onslaught will be drowned in a sea of blood. The turning point of the war will be decided by you."

After a quiet night they were attacked from the air, but the raid did not last long and afterwards they spent the rest of the day working on their positions, indeed, it was so quiet that they began to think that the enemy must have outflanked them. Then on the 18th it all began again:

"Suddenly a barrage of Stalin-Organ rockets descended on their position. They dived for cover at the bottom of the trench

s a hail of metal churned up the earth all round them in an unending petrifying in." Then the barrage subsided and all was quiet. But not for long. "'Stand to! The Russians are coming!' They grabbed their weapons and took up the allotted firing positions. German soldiers with Weimar armbands were running towards them these were renegade German troops who had changed sides and were now fighting for the Russians. They aimed and fired readily as they had been taught, aiming at the body."

The enemy attackers hesitated, then turned and ran. Clearly they had misjudged the strength of the defence, and also the ground, which undoubtedly favoured those in Lietzen rather than those attacking. Above all they had misjudged the defenders determination to fight on for the Führer.

Altner was both physically exhausted and in a state of shock after this encounter—the blood and the carnage, the death of his comrades (one in five of the company had been killed) had affected him badly. Also, he had not liked shooting at his own countrymen, it had distressed him greatly and after all, it was his first battle. Altner and Stroschn, however, had "come of age" in that short time, as can be judged by the fact that they quickly pulled themselves together and helped to bury the dead. Then they took up their positions again, while just behind them the Waffen-SS moved up to the village to ensure that the line held.

Nevertheless, the next major Soviet attack on the 20th was too strong. All they could do was to retreat. "Quickly, outside with your kit. The Russians are here!" And so they were—everywhere! Soon they were under a hail of bullets as machine gun and rifle fire swept the village. They were forced back through the village, which was now burning fiercely. The flames threatened to engulf them as they ran, but they were determined that nothing would stop them. One of Altner's comrades had a large piece

of shrapnel in his foot, but he ran on until he collapsed.

It was Hitler's birthday and the battalion commander announced that the British and Americans had signed a peace treaty the night before. He also told them that if they could only hold on for just 24 more hours, help would arrive—and they had believed him. In the morning they didn't know what to believe. "Dawn broke. The reality was full-scale rout." Battalion HQ was deserted and all around them was death and disaster. Just a few hundred metres to the east were the Russians, making swift progress, while to the west lay a long and dangerous path back to Berlin. The next village was Falkenhagen and the villagers stared in horror as their once proud and invincible army streamed past, broken. There were refugees also on the road, but they were ignored. On to Arensdorf, which had to be bypassed as it was engulfed in flames. As they approach Hasenfelde the church clock struck noon—it was 20 April the day of the major Russian breakthrough on the Oder Front.

Altner was still carrying all his equipment, unlike some of his comrades who had already ditched most of their gear. They were rapidly becoming exhausted and were also starving, so they stopped for food. He tells how a pig is killed at a nearby farm, then boiled, but before they could eat a mouthful, the enemy were seen on the horizon and their meal had to be abandoned! The road was agony on their feet, packstraps bit into their shoulders, while belts of ammunition banged painfully against their legs. They had covered some 48km by now and the two youngsters who had dropped behind, stopped for a rest, only to be surrounded by hysterical Hitler Youth: "Who are you? What do you want? Are you deserters?"

"Just food and rest. We're from the Oder Front and the Russians are coming, but they won't get here today." Bread to eat. Malt to drink. Tubs of cold water for bleeding feet. Straw for beds. Sleep.

They were awoken in the morning by loud explosions and the crashing of glass. They moved on quickly making for Rauen, a village to the south of the autobahn near Fürstenwalde. "Military Police were trying to control a mass of traffic converging on the autobahn, whilst the *Hitlerjugend* (Hitler Youth) and the *Volksturm* (Home Guard) worked frantically to improve the defences. Soldiers were marching along both sides of the road heading west as fully laden motor vehicles raced down the centre."

Soon they came to a bombed bridge, where a sergeant was directing traffic. He had propped up his bicycle a few yards away. The boys couldn't resist the temptation. Leaping on, with Altner pedalling and Stroschn on the carrier behind, they pedalled off furiously without being stopped! They kept on with just one short halt—to pick up a grubby salami that someone had dropped on the road (their breakfast!). All went well, they weren't chased, and they found the way to Rauen where they hoped they would meet up with the rest of their company. At the village crossroads they decided to split up to look for water. Stroschn was lucky and found the company almost at once, but two officious young officers stopped Altner. They confiscated the bike and, at gun point, ordered him to report to the barracks in nearby Fürstenwalde. Altner was really furious! He decided not to do as he had been ordered, so he pretended to go towards the barracks, then crept back and managed to get past them without being shot at. Then his luck changed. He, like Stroschn, met up with some of the company and so he was safe for a while—at least from German bullets, if not from the Russians!

"It was like being home again. It was good to be striding through the woods, led by Lt Fricke, a comfortable reassuring figure, and to be with all the others. The news was bad, but it did look as though they could get to Berlin if they moved quickly to Kummersdorf and got on a train due to leave that night. The ever resourceful Fricke even found an isolated farm for hot milk and a good supper. Then they piled into the goods train and fell asleep.

"Suddenly the wagon doors were wrenched open with a shout: 'Everybody out!' The Russians had blocked the line up ahead and now the only way forward was on foot. They piled out of the train despondently and marched off in single file, each man automatically placing one foot after the other, blindly following the man in front."

The company staggered on through the night, going through small villages where the Volkssturm were making half-hearted preparations for their defence—little use

against the mighty Red Army. Finally, they got to the station at Koenigs Wusterhausen, which was a large station on the Berlin line and probably represented the last chance of a train to safety. Unfortunately as they discovered, the station was deserted and the last train had left for Berlin hours ago. Morale hit rock bottom and they collapsed exhausted. Some of them were now in tears—was this the end? Fricke sensibly called a break and they slept.

Sleep revived them and the housewives of Koenigs Wusterhausen fed them, somehow, from their own meagre rations. Refreshed, they determined to have one final attempt to march the remaining 44km. Lt Fricke led them safely, by a circuitous route, and despite coming under direct attack at the Schoenfeld aerodrome, they survived. They stayed another night in an isolated farm, despite the farmer being scared and unwilling to help them as he was afraid what the approaching Russians would do when they arrived. However, he didn't really have much choice as they simply commandeered one of his barns. Three days they had been on the run—they had walked 180km and had another 25 to go. But again they got little sleep, being woken at 2300 hours with the news that the Russians were in the next village and coming their way!

"They marched on silently through the night each man engrossed in his own thoughts. The moon hung over the sleeping villages like a pale disc in the sky. The anti-tank barriers were closed, the cobbles dug up in places and anti-tank mines strewn in the ditches to catch the unwary. Sometimes a civilian sentry would accost them at the barricades they passed."

At long last they reached Lichtenrade, a suburb of Berlin—temporary safety for the 16 and 17-year olds, who now staggered along like pensioners. All they had to do now was to get to their barracks at Ruhleben on the northwest side of the city. They had made it, but Berlin was now a very strange place:

"Now here they could see Home Guard, mainly dressed in Waffen-SS camouflage uniforms, guarding the barricades and the Hitler Youth strutting around with their Panzerfäuste. SS were patrolling the streets in cars checking individual identities and occasionally picking someone up. Two SA men were standing smoking beside a lamp-post from which hung a tightly-bound man in civilian clothes, his dead eyes staring out of his blue face. A label pinned on his chest pronounced that he had been executed for cowardice and desertion. Altner felt sick. Was it all worth fighting for?"

The following day they received a new order to defend the suburb of Spandau. When they got to the northern outskirts of Spandau, they had to go along Niederneuendorfer Allee, then cut across a meadow to some trenches just by a deserted slave labour camp. As they ran through the meadow enemy machine guns and artillery fired them upon. Most of them made it to the trenches, only to find that they were unfinished and barely waist deep. One section was then ordered to cross a small track near to the rear of the labour camp. Altner followed this section as it was his job, as a runner, to liaise between this advance group and the main body. Just then an enemy tank appeared and started shooting at them, killing all but two of the advanced section. The sergeant, who was armed with the only Panzerfaust, was killed before he could use it. Somehow Altner managed to get back to the main trench safely. Then:

"...there was the roar of an engine and the rattling of tracks from the right flank where a massive tank emerged from the trees. The Staff Sergeant called for a Panzerfaust but there were none available. The gun dipped and fired along the length of the trench. Only Altner had any cover, being round a slight bend next to the labour camp. The gun kept on firing methodically destroying the trench and killing its occupants. Someone tried to run but was immediately gunned down by the tank's machine gun ... The survivors started crawling back through the dead and dying while enemy fire continued unabated over their heads."

Stroschn, Altner's pal, was killed. Altner survived and made his way back to a cellar in the centre of Spandau, and spent the night weeping like a baby. There were a few attempts to defend some of the buildings in Spandau, but most of the company had lost their will to fight and the suburb was evacuated on 26 April. Just before withdrawing over the Charlotte Bridge they heard a Red Army propaganda broadcast, telling them that Berlin was surrounded and that there was no escape.

They managed to get back to their barracks at Ruhleben and to barricade it against the attack that they expected from Spandau. When it came the Russians stormed the rear of the barracks and Altner found himself fighting in the same practice training area where he had carried out his training. And it was here that Altner was, for the first and only time, involved in a battle against the Red Army when he was on the winning side. He was in one of the practice trenches, along with some Hitler Youth, partly trained recruits, even some women, all of whom were firing at the enemy. Then a Russian tank appeared with a white flag and broadcast a message:

"Comrades, give yourselves up. There is no point in continuing to fight. The Russian have you covered and the barracks are completely surrounded. Run over and repor to the Russian troops on the Reichssportfeld You will be well treated and as soon a hostilities have ended you will be allowed t go home. Soldiers there is no point in it any more. Do you want to die in the last hours o a war that is already lost?"

This appeal caused some of those in th trenches to get up and run in the directio of the sports field, but they were mainl shot in the back by their erstwhil comrades still in the trenches. Altner di not run and instead he found himself takin part in his very first counterattack. It wa exhilarating to be advancing at long las and he was sad that Stroschn wasn't wit him. They advanced across the trainin ground under heavy fire. However, th impediments of the obstacle course, th houses in the mock village that had bee used to train for street fighting all provide cover and made it extremely difficult for th enemy to hit them. This hodgepodge o several hundred ill-assorted Germa soldiers surprisingly pushed the Russia back into the woods and even out of th suburbs around the barracks. The Russian were very surprised by this unexpecte resistance and lost many troops. Helmut Altner was pleased to have taken part.

Altner would eventually be captured b the Russians near Weseram some 10k west of Berlin. He and some others ha been trying to escape, again walking fo ages, almost to the point of shee exhaustion. Then they heard a Sovie armoured car and had hidden from successfully.

"They were so tired they could scarcel move but they forced themselves on . Suddenly they heard voices calling behin them and looking back, they saw th Russians. They started running in pan towards the haven of the woods but firin broke out and bullets started flying a around them. They carried on running bu the Russians were gaining rapidly, Altne who was out of breath, stopped and thre his pistol away. It was over, the Russian were all round them. They led him back the road. Altner, who had an injured fo stumbled. A Russian soldier picked him u steadied him and gave him a cigarett Altner burst into tears."

Right: These two young Hitler Youth "boy soldiers" were captured by the US 11th Armored Division of Patton's Third Army; many of the same age tried to stop the Red Army in the streets of Berlin. (US Army)

Battle in the Snow

Main Picture: Approach march through the snow. (All photos in this section *H-G. Sandmann*)

Above: The company pushes on.

Right: A pause to check bearings.

Below: Sleighs at the rear with essential supplies.

Bottom: Into the village . . .

Left: The mortars lay down a barrage on the retreating enemy.

Below: Check every house.

Bottom: Smoke from burning houses obscures part of the village.

Above: Flak defence is set up as the battalion consolidates.

Right: The enemy dead surround the village.

Below: Some prisoners are taken.

Chapter 13
Taken Prisoner and POW

Left: "Kamerad!" This 14-year old sniper was captured by the Americans in Coutances, near St. Lô. (US Army)

Battle Group 981 from the remnants of the regiment, reinforced by some soldiers who had been brought in by the Field Police. They were a mixed bunch—men from all kinds of units with little equipment, some of them even unarmed. They were a complete unknown and didn't trust each other. We marched on from Oberdreis, to get into action somewhere—nobody could tell us where exactly! They told us we would find the front without any problem: 'You only have to follow the sounds of battle,' because it had been written in Generalfeldmarschall Model's order to stand fast. We all had to sign that order, which told us that: 'Anyone who retreats from the front will get the death sentence by hanging!'

"We went from Wilroth via the autobahn to the area of Waldbreitach on the River Wied. The road runs along the left side of the river and has steep rocks along its side, with a bridge that leads in the direction of Hausen. Over here we found a bottleneck situation, everyone was making for this bridge to get across, while the enemy artillery was coming in and enemy aircraft filled the sky overhead. Bombs and shells hit the rocks behind the bridge and their effect on the men waiting to cross was terrible—it was a race against death to get to the other side. We waited for the right moment to run across the bridge—again we had losses. Our wounded were brought to a nearby cloister, which also had 'Hospital' clearly marked on its walls. An old man and a young boy were lying on the bridge when I ran across.

"We took shelter from the enemy planes in the church of the village. It was a game of 'cat and mouse' in which the enemy planes chased us around the church several times. I almost got hit when machine gun bullets missed me by only a few inches, their impact spraying dirt in my face. Then we marched on via Hausen and Frohath, we could now clearly hear the increasing sounds of battle. We took up positions in a patch of woodland at the village of Weissfeld. The 14th March passed quietly enough, then on the 15th around noon we saw Americans in front of our positions.

To be taken prisoner in battle by the Allies during World War II must undoubtedly have been viewed as an automatic safe conduct pass to a new and easier life. However, the brutal facts were that people did not always survive the experience. Although accurate figures are not always easy to come by, it has been estimated that of the 3,155,000 German servicemen of all ranks, who were taken prisoner by the Soviets, a harrowing 1,185,000 died in captivity. Of those captured by the Western Allies, the most fortunate were the ones in British hands, because the French, on the whole, did not treat their prisoners particularly well and several thousand died of disease. The Americans, who had the misfortune to have to look after the bulk of the German POWs, did not have enough resources to back up their intended POW system, and thus lost some 100,000 through death by neglect by 1946. (Source: *World War Two—Nation by Nation* by J. Lee Ready)

Otto Gunkel of 272 VGD had been fighting all through the Ardennes offensive. Now at the end of February, 1945, the tide had turned completely, the winter was over and the enemy was counter-attacking strongly. His division took heavy losses and were forced to retreat as he recalls:

"The Americans broke through our defences in many places on March 3. Their tanks, which hadn't been much use in the hills of the Eifel, now rolled unhindered through the open plains via Euskirchen and Rheinbach to reach the Rhine river. We defended desperately, but often the enemy tanks had already bypassed us ... We had managed an orderly retreat via Scheuren, Altenhar and Ahrweiler to the Rhine River, which we reached on 7 March. The American tanks were already at the Remagen Bridge and had established a bridgehead there on the same day. From this bridgehead they would push deeper into Germany. We marched upstream along the Rhine, trying to find a safe place to cross. All the roads that were coming from the Eifel and on the west side of the river were clogged with retreating German troops. Fortunately the cloudy, foggy weather prevented the enemy aircraft getting into action, otherwise it would have caused thousands of deaths on the roads.

"We crossed the Rhine over the railway bridge at Engers during the night. Then for the next two days we were at Isenburg in the Westerwald, where the remnants of our division rallied again. It had been a long, long way through the Eifel and my boots were completely worn out. They set up

Right: A young Nazi soldier surrenders on the outskirts of St Lô, 20 July 1944. (*US Army*)

Right: One of the "biggest" prisoners taken (in every sense of the word—he was known by some as *Der Dicke* [Fatty] as he weighed over 20 stone!)—was Reichsmarschall Hermann Goering, who surrendered to US 36th Infantry Division in Austria, near Mauterndorf on 8 May 1945. (*US Army*)

They didn't attack us but rather pushed through on the left of our positions towards Frohath. That evening our company commander told me to try to locate the Battalion Command Post, which had been in a quarry between Hoenningen and Frohath. There I would receive fresh orders.

"It must have been around 1900 hours, not far from this quarry, when I ran straight into a group of American infantrymen. When I heard: 'Hands Up!' I dropped my 98k rifle and raised my hands. Resistance was useless and would have been suicide. I was a prisoner of war."

"On 5 March 1945, our group, after the last push, was taken prisoner by the Americans. We were searched and had many things taken from us that we never got back."

Rolf Werner Voelker was another German infantryman, captured by the Amis, and his treatment was not perhaps what he had expected.

"We were beginning to think that it must be concentrated hatred or so-called revenge, because I have never come across such an undignified way to handle human beings as in that POW camp. One thing they did was to fill a stocking with sand and start hitting us with it. And they were not particular where they hit you. This happened to me in Saarburg by the Americans. I was hit in the kidneys so hard that for weeks I had pain and my urine was nearly black with blood. This 'joke' cost me a kidney. In Trier, it was also normal to hit the prisoners on their bandages, where they had been wounded. Then on the lorry through Luxembourg and also in an open coal wagon on the railway, through France, the people through stones at us, sometimes dung and on the bridges they urinated over us.

"At Maillee le Camp, south of Charlon sur Marne, we began our 're-education' to democracy. We were shown photographs of the concentration camps that had been

liberated and I tried to comprehend the scenes. I had seen most of the big cities in Germany destroyed—so many wives, mothers and children killed or burnt in the air raids, but I could not believe these photographs—or rather, I did not want to believe them.

"The punishment there was severe, when you made a mistake you were made to stand for hours in the heat of the day without anything on your head, sleep in something like a cage on stony ground with just two blankets—one to sleep on the other to cover you up. I was not very well liked by the Amis, but they gave me a job—to find out who was stealing food out of the kitchens, the Polish guards or the people who were working in the kitchen, all were under suspicion.

"In June 1945, I was detailed to help build a new part of the camp for the men who were going to be discharged first. I was promoted to take charge of the new place, c

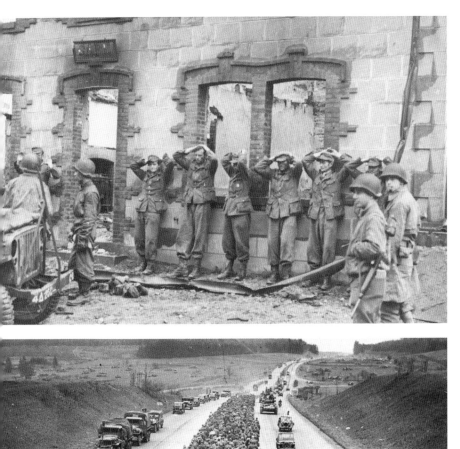

Left: German prisoners under guard. They have lost arms and equipment, but at least they know that they are safely in the hands of the US Army and not the Russians. (US Army)

Left: German prisoners walk along the centre island of the autobahn near Giesen, while Sherman tanks and other vehicles of the US 6th Armored Division roll past them. (US Army)

sort of camp policeman. The first to be discharged were the miners, postmen, railway workers and farmers. As I have said before, I had many differences of opinion with the officer in charge of the camp, so I was surprised when they gave me a good reference. However, I can honestly say that I truly was reliable and trustworthy.

"The house of my parents was in the French zone [sic: of the divided Germany], so I thought it would be better to go to Stuttgart, because I was afraid they might arrest me again. I went back to a ruin of a house that once had been my home. Most of Stuttgart was flat and the people were living all together like rabbits in any hole that was empty. Supplies were very bad, but on the Black Market you could buy anything. You did not need any money, just cigarettes. Without cigarettes no food. At this time people were beginning to lose their morality ... hunger and misery were the everyday life. The people accepted this

misery, but still with bitterness... For the first two years after the war, in winter, in the ruins of the city, it was almost impossible to live. The only suit I possessed was my old uniform that had been dyed a different colour and two sets of underclothing, nothing else. My two days food ration (bread) was eaten in one day. In this miserable situation I registered for a job with an American Engineer regiment. At this time I was reluctant to work for any army. It was dangerous work, clearing mines. The only reason for doing this job was that we got one good meal a day. On the border area between the French and American zones, where the German Army had been way back in 1945, they had destroyed some of the mines but there were many forgotten and most of them had trip wires attached, so they were very dangerous.

"Eventually my wife to be, Erika, found me again. Her family had escaped from the

Russians to Austria in May 1945, but Czech partisans had shot her sister Gerda. Austria was once again a free country. I had been over the border many times and could have landed in prison, but now I didn't have to take the risk any more. With the new money in 1948 there was more food on the market. I started again in a job in October as a mechanic in Esslingen. The work was very hard. We fished out steel girders and other useful material from bomb damaged buildings to use for rebuilding, working seventy hours a week—but we took Sunday off for a game of football!"

Rolf goes on to tell how Erika and he were eventually married, how he had a successful career and a very happy marriage until her unfortunate death in 1994. He closes his reminiscences with the words, which have been echoed by so many of the old soldiers who have contributed their memories to this book:

"In the future, I will keep on working for freedom and for a better understanding, just as well and hard as I can."

Hubert Gees, who was taken prisoner by the Americans at the village of Hürtgen on 28 November 1944 recalled how:

"After we had spent the night in a cellar of a house in Roetgen, we were taken to a POW camp at Welkenrath, Belgium on the 29th, where we saw a lot of tents in a muddy field. On the 30th they brought us to the American War Cemetery at Henri Chapelle, where we had to dig graves. The next evening we were put on to a freight train. During the night I peeped out through a hole in the wagon and saw that we were at Huy in Belgium. The next day, 1 December 1944, we arrived at another POW camp, close to the railway lines at Namur, Belgium. I can remember that it was a large reddish-brown building with only a few windows. Then, on Sunday, 3 December, they loaded us onto another freight train during a heavy snowfall and took us to a POW camp at Compiègne, France, we arrived there in the afternoon of 4 December.

"There would be a long way, full of uncertainty, to go until I would finally be released from POW camp in January, 1947—a long way until I could go home. 'It's good that people don't know in advance what is going to happen.' That is often said after bad experiences. That also goes for war and for imprisonment—but if a man doesn't lose his will to survive, he can stand much more than an animal.

"We Germans cannot turn back the clock and make the German war crimes that were committed and the Holocaust undone. That is why it must be our special duty to all victims of the war, to promote peace and to work for understanding between our nations and for reconciliation over the graves. That should be the mission for all us survivors."

Above left: Some of the German POWs who reached England. These newly arrived prisoners are being searched once again on their arrival in Portland, Dorset. (US National Archives)

Left: Into the stockade. Thousands of German POWs were herded into stockades for checking and counting. (US Army)

Right: "Where have all the young men gone? Gone to graveyards every one." (H-G. Sandmann)

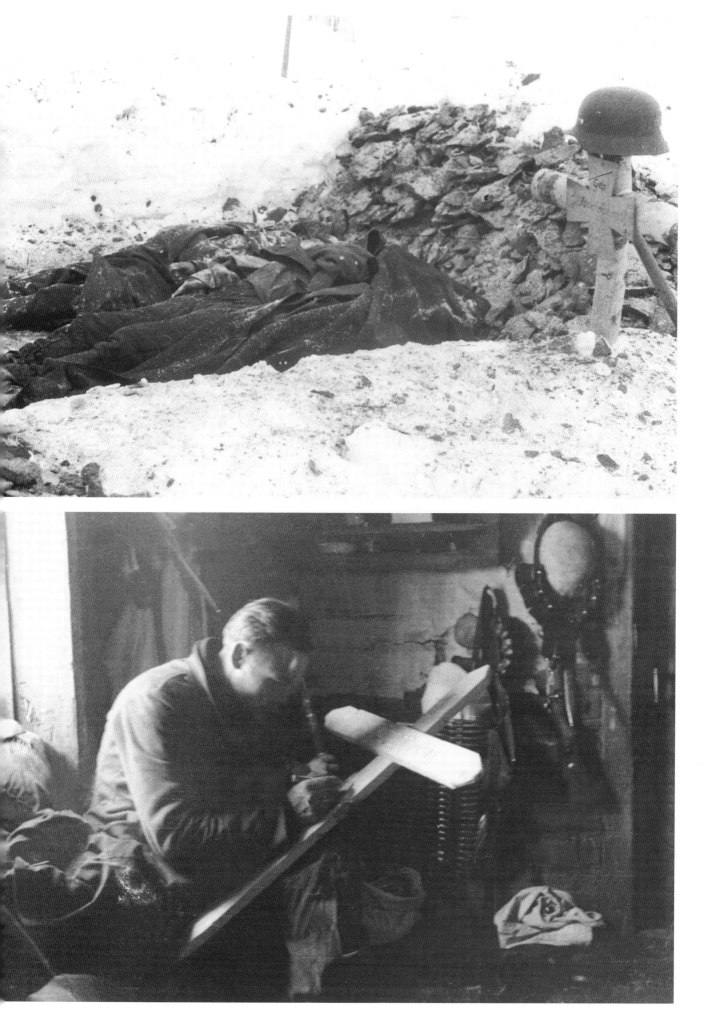

Bibliography

Aufsess, Baron von: *The von Aufsess Occupation Diary*; Phillimore, 1985.

Forty, George: *The Fall of France*; Nutshell Publishing, 1990.

Forty, George: *Afrika Korps at War*; Ian Allan Publishing, 1978.

Forty, George; *The Armies of Rommel*; Cassell (Arms & Armour Press), 1997

Horne, Alistair: *To Lose a Battle—France 1940*; Macmillan, 1969.

Le Tissier, A. H. (ed.): *Berlin Soldier* (edited translation and abridgement of Altner H, *Totentanz Berlin* 1947, Berlin Bulletin 1985); Jonathan Cape, 1988.

Mitcham, Samuel W.: *Hitler's Legions*; Leo Cooper, 1985.

Ready, J. Lee: *World War Two, Nation by Nation*; Arms & Armour, 1995.

Schmidt, Heinz Werner: *With Rommel in the Desert*; George G. Harrap & Co Ltd, 1951. (Copyright holder is now Eric Dobby Publishing Ltd.)

REFERENCE WORKS

Dept of the Army Pamphlet No 20-269—*HISTORICAL STUDY—SMALL UNIT ACTIONS DURING THE GERMAN CAMPAIGN IN RUSSIA*, July 1953.

Balkenkreuz über Wüstensand—Farbbilderwerk vom Deutschen Afrikakorps; Gerhard Stalling Verlag, 1943.

War Diary of No 8 MG Bn, 1 Pz Gren Regt Die 1 (H) 14 Pz in Westen 1940.

IWM SOUND ARCHIVE TAPES
No 13146—OTL Karl Günther von Hase
No 10006/8—Erwin Grubba

Below: The epitome of the Eastern Front—a German infantry column presses on through the everlasting forests cloaked in thick snow. (H-G. Sandmann)